# JUST DO YOU

Authenticity, Leadership, and Your Personal Brand

LISA KING

*Published by Ingenium Books Publishing Inc.*

*Toronto, Ontario, Canada M6P 1Z2*



ingeniumbooks.com



*ISBNs*

*Paperback: 978-1-989059-35-7*

*eBook: 978-1-989059-34-0*

*Hardcover: 978-1-989059-36-4*

*Audiobook: 978-1-989059-37-1*

Author photo: Keegan Evans Photography

Graphic Design: Heidi Hackler, Dolphin Design

Cover Design: Lisa King and Andrew King

# Contents

*For Aiden*

*Your spirit and energy light up any room.*
*Remember that being yourself*
*is the best thing you can ever be.*
*Chase your dreams: you have the power*
*and potential to make them your reality.*
*You are a leader who will surely change the world.*

# Praise for Lisa King

This is much more than a book about leadership! This is a book of self-discovery. You will discover the person you are and learn how that can be translated into the best version of you as a leader. It's a powerful road map to bringing out the leader inside of you.

Bill Colombo, former president and COO, Dick's Sporting Goods

*Just Do You* offers important strategies for life as well as career. Having worked with Lisa and experienced her talent, it is wonderful to see her empowering lessons on the personal brand each of us has, brought together in a narrative that is truly life changing. Take the action. Believe in yourself. Are you ready to achieve excellence? Buy the book!

Kathy Ireland, chair and CEO, kathy ireland Worldwide

Personal brands can be powerful, especially when they are driven by purpose. The exercises and collection of stories act as a compass to map a direct course of action, to raise the bar in all we do, lead with authenticity and purpose, and create a strong personal brand.

Adam Weitsman, CEO, Upstate Shredding

*Just Do You* is a powerful and compelling book that allows each of us to explore how to be our authentic selves. Lisa has crafted an easy-to-follow framework and guide for self-reflection, to identify how to *Just Do You.* This is a must read for people looking to create their own brand in a way that enables their authenticity, and for them and those that surround them to shine and thrive. Congratulations Lisa on distilling authenticity to a guide for all of us to benefit from.

Laura Guggenheim, vice president of national sales, Procter & Gamble

Having had the privilege of working side-by-side with Lisa for a decade and a half, I know, first-hand, that she practices what she preaches. Putting her behaviors into this work is a gift to all of us striving to be our best leader selves. The world is starving for authentic leadership in this age where media and marketing dominate how we think and, ultimately, act. Her work is timely. If you lead now, or are preparing to become a leader, this book is essential. Read on to find your *true north* and let your uniqueness shine. The world needs what you have.

David Casullo, author of *Leading the High Energy Culture*

Great leadership starts from a platform of solid self-understanding. Lisa King's book, *Just Do You* provides the tools to achieve something that goes beyond the intuitive notions we have of ourselves. It encourages us to take chances and look at ourselves from all angles. This is important work. It's not easy but Lisa takes us through the process in a helpfully structured way. Read the book. Get the workbook. Do the work. You'll be glad you did.

Gwyn Teatro, author, *In the Thick of It: Mastering the Art of Leading From the Middle.*

To be yourself in a world that is constantly trying to make you something else is the greatest accomplishment.

Ralph Waldo Emerson

# Introduction

Leaders have tremendous influence. They can affect the way others think, feel, and contribute. Unfortunately, when they don't lead with authenticity and purpose, many leaders fall short.

There's a significant difference between a boss and a leader. Many people are promoted to management positions but aren't ready or equipped to lead, perhaps due to lack of training, lack of clarity around expectations, or even uncertainty about effective leadership behaviors. Sometimes good people get caught up in a negative culture and model the bad behaviors of other bosses. And sometimes people aren't clear about what they value and consequently lose their way.

Several years ago, I was the newest member of a small executive leadership team in a growing organization, surrounded by leaders whose tenure far surpassed my own. For some, the company was all they knew—they'd never worked anywhere else. The culture was well established, highly competitive, and executive leaders were dominating. The company was growing as a result of earning new customers. In fact, it was aggressively hiring new employees in all functional areas of the business, including mine.

One of the employees I hired was an energetic, appropriately assertive, and highly intelligent young man. Let's call him Ben. Ben was eager to learn, prove himself, and grow quickly in the organization. For the first year, he worked closely with me, always sought feedback on how to improve, and genuinely wanted to do his best. People liked Ben. He was friendly and supportive. He regularly added significant value to the work, and was easy to work with.

As a rising star, Ben quickly gained the trust of customers. The executive leadership team wanted to increase his responsibilities, and I agreed wholeheartedly. So, we expanded his scope of work, allowing him to work directly with the CEO and other leaders on the executive team. This gave Ben a boost of confidence. Eager to prove himself, and his sights set on a promotion, Ben began to closely watch the behaviors of some of the executives and the CEO. He observed their actions in meetings, how they directed other employees, and their communication styles—and he began to model their behaviors.

As a result, Ben became highly competitive with his peers. He dominated in meetings, barked directions at fellow employees when collaborating on projects, and shot off abrupt emails, often forgetting to say "Thank you." Ben's stress level also rose significantly. It was apparent to me that he was in conflict with himself.

I received complaints from the CEO and a few of the other executives. They felt Ben's behavior had become abrasive and was negatively affecting the staff. They were completely blind to the fact that Ben was modeling *their* behaviors to impress them and get a promotion. After all, they represented success, right?

Unfortunately, conflict like Ben's is common in many organizations. When his modeled behaviors and professional goals conflicted with who he was as a person, he became physically exhausted and mentally stressed. He couldn't see a way to achieve what he needed professionally while remaining *himself* in the organization.

I encouraged Ben to clarify what mattered to him and to realign his behaviors, goals, and core values so they were consistent. In time, people once again began to see Ben for who he really was, and with a renewed focus, he got that well-deserved promotion.

Ben is now happier and remains true to himself. He still has some difficult days, but he regularly reminds himself what really matters. He's focused on investing in himself and his future in ways that will drive success—likely in another organization where the culture is a better fit.

Ben's story is true, but like some of the other stories involving real people that I've included throughout this book, I've changed his name.

*Just Do You* will help you gain an understanding of your authentic leadership style, get clear on your personal brand, help you gain the confidence to live *your* brand, and challenge you to make your mark on the world.

Connecting with the authentic leader in you begins with exploring what matters deeply to you. When you're clear about what matters and have done the self-discovery work to better understand what leadership means to you, then—and only then—are you truly ready to authentically lead. All your experiences and influences have created an image in your head and a feeling in your soul about leadership. As you work through the exercises in *Just Do You*, you'll dig deeper into your feelings about leadership to determine what kind of leader you are and what kind of leader you want to become.

Once you're clear on what matters and what that means in terms of your personal brand, you can focus on honing your leadership skills in all of your personal and professional relationships. The stories in this book will help you see the difference between effective leaders and leaders who harm or hinder others. Leaders create great experiences for others when authenticity and purpose are evident.

I have one simple goal for *Just Do You*: to share my knowledge and experience; to pay it forward by giving the gift that was given to me by all the great leaders in my life. I want to empower you to become the most authentic version of yourself and to encourage you to lead. If you've been struggling with leadership, are seeking clarity about who you are, aren't prioritizing what's really important in your life, or questioning your life's purpose, this book is for you.

You won't find me disputing the leadership skill-building methodologies of other thought-leaders. In fact, I believe the methodology shared in *Just Do You* builds a foundation so that leadership skill-building can be achieved once your authentic personal brand emerges. You will recognize what is or isn't working today and gain the tools to define *your* leadership style—in alignment with *your* purpose.

Throughout my nearly thirty-year career in marketing, branding, and leader development, I have witnessed the power and influence of inspirational, authentic leaders, as well as the drain and harm caused by ineffective bosses. As I reflect on my career, the greatest reward and measure of success has come from the relationships I've built and from the privilege of leading and developing leaders. When young leaders realize their potential, gain confidence, and accomplish more than they thought was possible, it brings me tremendous joy. They become a part of something larger than themselves and bring great value to a team and organization.

My interest in connecting leadership authenticity to personal branding began during my time as senior vice president of marketing at Raymour & Flanigan Furniture. Former Raymour & Flanigan senior vice president of human resources, David Casullo (now my business partner, CEO of Daneli Partners, and author of *Leading the High Energy Culture*), had launched the Leadership Development Institute and was creating programs for leaders at all levels in the organization. I approached him with the idea of creating a personal branding training module based on the business-branding methodology I'd applied throughout my marketing career. I expressed my desire to help others discover their authentic brand. Dave wholeheartedly agreed, the personal branding program was created, and I delivered it to hundreds of Raymour & Flanigan associates.

The program has evolved over the years. And I've committed myself to teaching this methodology and empowering the next generation of leaders—like you—to live their brand and lead with authenticity and purpose. Why? Because I see the impact this process can have on a person. I see the positive ripple effect authentic leaders have on others. I want to help anyone who is willing and determined to live their brand in alignment with what matters most to them.

The exercises in *Just Do You* will challenge you to become aware of what matters to you, and connect with these principles. You'll learn about the power of branding. You'll learn how to determine if your personal brand is reflected the way you intend. You'll become clear on how your true brand intersects with what matters. As a result, you'll see how you can lead with authenticity and build influence. You'll gain the tools to confidently live, behave, and share your unique brand with the world.

Once you're living your unique personal brand, recognizing when you connect with a person, a job, a community, a cause, or an organization, becomes easier. You'll have a True North. It'll make a course of action clearer. Your True North allows you to see what's worth working toward, and what's worth walking away from. It provides you with a strong sense of purpose, a critical aspect of overall happiness.

Through conscious consideration and personal experiences, I have come to know and understand my personal brand. I strive to live and lead in a manner that is consistent with it. This has helped me navigate difficult decisions because I have a True North, a fixed point that orients me in a spinning world. It's my internal compass, helping me stay focused on the right direction. My True North is a result of who I am at my core. When something doesn't fit who I am, this inner compass tells me I'm off course. I know I need to change course soon, but in the meantime, I need to be authentic and true to myself through the challenging experience. I once heard someone say, "Do you want that [person] [job] [situation] to be in the next chapter of your book? If not, then take control of your book and write a new chapter!" That wise advice has guided me many times in my life.

*Just Do You* can produce the same results for you.

I've divided *Just Do You* into four key parts:

- In Part One, *The Leader in You*, we'll examine what authentic leadership looks like and what gaps exist today. Then, you'll explore what leadership means to you by reflecting on the experiences and people who shaped you, who you are and what's most important to you, the things that motivate you, and the goals you strive for.

- Part Two, *Brands and Why They Matter*, begins with an introduction to branding as it relates to people and businesses. You'll learn about the six attributes of brands and how to rate authenticity. Next, you'll activate what matters to you by aligning it with your brand attributes. At the end of this section, you will have a clear picture of your current personal brand and your True North.

- In Part Three, *Your True North*, you'll identify conflicts and discover ways to return to your True North when life unexpectedly throws you off track. You will learn which aspects of your brand you control and how to rebound when something happens that you cannot control.

- Part Four, *Your Time to Lead*, ties it all together by providing examples of what matters in authentic leadership. It will challenge you to tap into the power of your unique strengths. With clarity (of your purpose) and an understanding of what matters, you will be empowered to take the necessary steps forward.

Some chapters have questions for you to put the process into practice. Visit www.danelipartners.com/books/justdoyou to get your companion workbooks for this book so you can capture your responses.

Although the process you are about to embark upon may make you a bit uncomfortable, as you seek to understand yourself and your personal brand, rest assured, a leader will emerge. Use the lessons and exercises in this book to open your mind to think differently about leadership. Throughout this book, you'll hear stories from leaders who share what matters most to them, and stories from followers who share what leadership qualities and behaviors resonate most. As a result, you'll discover that you have the power and potential to lead inside you. You can lead with authenticity by taking control of your words and actions to ensure they're in alignment with what matters to you and is a clear reflection of your personal brand.

Are you ready to become the kind of leader you wish you had? It doesn't matter where you're starting from. You have the power to lead. It may seem like a daunting challenge, but you picked this book for a reason. The world needs authentic leaders.

It's time for you to make your mark, lead, and impact the world—to just do you! Let's begin.

# Part One

## The Leader in You

## Chapter 1

# Authentic Leadership

> *If your actions inspire others to dream more, learn more, do more, and become more, you are a leader.*
>
> John Quincy Adams

I'm going to challenge you to reconsider what you believe about leadership. In this chapter, I'll share examples of leaders, expose the gaps in modern leadership, and provide examples of behaviors that work against leaders. You'll begin to think differently about who the authentic leaders are in your life.

In this chapter, you'll learn:

- What it means to step up and lead

- Why authenticity matters
- What the leadership gap is and how you can help fill it

## Who is a Leader?

It can be difficult for young, impressionable leaders to determine what characteristics will guide them to success. Most will look to people who have risen to the ranks of executive leadership and say, "Well, they *must* have what it takes. After all, they hold the title I want someday."

Leadership can be confusing. It's easy to conclude that to succeed, you must model someone else's behaviors and *become* like them. But modeling behaviors won't get you to a place of authenticity. People will see through these behaviors and lose trust and faith in your leadership abilities. However, by observing the leaders in your life, you can assess which behaviors have either a positive or a negative impact on others. These observations can help you determine what authenticity looks like in another leader—and what inauthenticity looks like.

Authentic leadership comes from the heart and represents who you are and what you believe. Your actions embody these things.

The world needs authentic leaders. Leaders have the power and potential to influence and change the world. And leadership isn't reserved for those who hold a specific title or have an impressive educational background; each of us has the potential to lead.

Leaders step up, step in, and step forward with authenticity and purpose. They stand out and draw attention. Leaders are clear about who they are and what they care about. Leaders influence others in meaningful and lasting ways.

When I think about people whose authenticity has inspired me—encouraged me to do more and dream more—and the people who stood out when circumstances required them to, I think of many different people, not just people who hold titles in business.

When I was eight years old, my grandfather told me, "You're going to do something special." I believed him. Though he was an executive at IBM, he cherished his roles as a husband, father, and grandfather. I was only ten when we lost him, and I've thought about his encouraging words ever since. In times of success, I've smiled and felt proud, knowing he was right. In times of struggle and failure, his words have fueled me. I've learned to grow from each failure and take away the positives so I won't make the same mistakes twice. I've learned to dream big because my grandfather made me believe I could. My grandfather was a leader.

I started my marketing career at Dick's Sporting Goods right out of college. My manager, Bill, who was in his early thirties, mentored me and gave me opportunities I didn't believe I was ready for. He had a profound and lasting impact on me. In addition to helping me gain the skills and competencies necessary for my roles, he bolstered my confidence and made me feel comfortable with stretching, failing, and learning. He consistently pushed me outside my comfort zone until eventually my comfort zone expanded. Bill is an amazing listener who learns what motivates his employees. His influence is broad and his authenticity shines through in every interaction with his employees. He's more than whatever title he holds. Bill is a leader.

My lifelong friend Heather suffered a traumatizing health scare in her forties. After a few years of navigating the difficult situation and working hard to regain her health, she reflected on the lessons learned from this low point in her life. Heather realized that her experience had enabled her to help others overcome the kind of adversity she'd endured. She's always been caring and helpful, but her traumatic experience inspired her to share her story and connect deeply with others facing similar challenges. Now, the list of people, young and old, whom she mentors is long. Heather makes time for each person, listens thoughtfully, cares deeply, and supports them through their struggles. Her dedication, deep faith, and compassion for others defines her. She always lifts people up and inspires them. Heather is a leader.

When I was in an executive position later in my career, a young woman named Amanda joined my team in an entry-level position. Until that point, I'd never met anyone more prepared for an interview. And I've interviewed a lot of people! Amanda studied the job description and came prepared with well-thought-out questions. She'd researched the company and what it did, and she'd also carefully reviewed my LinkedIn profile—she asked me questions about my marketing career and experiences. After she was hired, Amanda jumped on the speeding train and learned quickly. She was always the first one to take on more. She embraced each opportunity to grow, even if the work fell outside her job description. She wanted to demonstrate her skills and broaden her influence by working on as many different projects with as many people as possible. Amanda's work ethic was infectious—those around her were inspired to learn more and do more as a result. Amanda is a leader.

My friend and colleague, Sara, has a son named Michael. Michael is obsessed with sports. He frequently surprises his mother with his knowledge of players, stats, and details about games long before he was born. When Michael was nine years old, Sara shared this story on Facebook: "Michael is reading *Think Like a Warrior: The Five Inner Beliefs That Make You Unstoppable*, by Darrin Donnelly. He's about halfway through. After his football game today, he told me how much he's learned from it already. 'Mom, we were playing football and my team was down a lot. I pulled them in and told them to embrace what's important now, not ten minutes ago. Well, Mom, they embraced it and we ended up winning!' he said." Michael is a leader.

In the summer of 2018, my mother was ill and frequently in the hospital. My father, my sisters, and I faced some difficult circumstances. Watching a loved one deteriorate before your eyes is heart-wrenching. Often, I was overcome with emotion and found it difficult to think clearly. Even through her own grief, my daughter, Jessica, who's a social worker, rose to the occasion—she got involved. She talked to the hospital staff and helped my father navigate the system to get the services and home aids he needed to care for my mother. She was calm, direct, and took care of everything. I was amazed and proud. She stepped up in those last few weeks of my mother's life. Jessica is a leader.

You can be a leader at any age, and you can develop your leadership skills over time, through life experiences. Everyone has the power to inspire others to dream more, learn more, do more, and become more. Your unique leadership skills are gifts worth sharing with the world.

## What Makes a Leader Authentic?

The best leaders, the authentic leaders, are true to themselves, to their values, and to what they believe. And these truths are evident in the experiences they create with others. Their authenticity shines through in everything they do. It motivates, inspires, and influences others. Authentic leaders provide encouragement and direction, and they're crystal clear about their role: to help others grow and develop. Leaders support their staff, their peers, and other leaders. They set an example.

Authentic leaders are clear about who they are—their identity. They know their personal brand, and live it proudly. They align their efforts and relationships in order to fulfill their purpose. This may sound difficult or idealistic, but it's not. Being yourself is actually the easiest thing you can do. When people see the genuine you, they'll be more likely to follow you, and to be inspired to pursue their own purpose.

## The Leadership Gap

There are a few ways to think about the leadership gap. Simply put, the leadership gap occurs when leaders aren't meeting the needs of their followers or their organizations.

Sometimes there's a gap between a leader's competency and the position they hold. There could also be a gap between their authenticity and behavior. Then, there's the gap between what employees want and need from their leaders.

Authenticity and purpose always trump skill, regardless of how new a leader is to a role. People will rally around someone who is building skills while remaining open to feedback. Trust is built as the leader and their team begin to collaborate and work toward common goals. Conversely, people will reject the arrogant leader who relies on title instead of authenticity. This leader will lose the team's respect, and their skill gap will be much more obvious. The team will disengage and point out the leader's weaknesses.

Neil was one of the most authentic and effective leaders I had the privilege of working with. He relied on his team and empowered us to be our best selves. Neil didn't behave as if he were the smartest person in the room, even though he held the position of CEO in a successful company. He knew he didn't know everything. He leveraged his team of executives and required each of us to be experts in our fields. Neil's purpose in terms of the company was clear: to create the best possible customer experience in the industry. We all knew what mattered to Neil. He cared deeply about his family, his customers, and his employees, and this was evident in every decision he made. Neil was firm but fair, and not one of us wanted to disappoint him—ever. As a team, we shared ideas, debated, and strategized. Neil supported us if we felt strongly about an initiative. He'd ask tough questions to test our resolve and ensure we did our homework. And when Neil decided on a specific direction, we all rallied behind him and forged ahead as a unified team. His authenticity and leadership inspired us to stretch and grow.

Sam, another leader I worked with, was a contrast to Neil. (Sam isn't his real name.) Sam was elevated to a role without the necessary experience, skills, or knowledge. Sam *did* behave as if he were the smartest person in the room. He led each meeting as though he were holding court. Sam's way was always the best way. Many of Sam's staff were older than he was, yet he chose not to draw on their wisdom and expertise. Perhaps he feared they would diminish his power. When senior team members tried to interject during meetings, Sam began inviting to meetings only those team members he felt he could control. This tactic caused many on his team to disengage and complain about his lack of leadership skills. They questioned his authority and whether his values aligned with the company's. Sam's leadership style—bossing versus leading—caused the team to unravel. It was unclear what his purpose was other than wanting to boss the team around and impose his prestigious new title on us. As a result, many left the organization disillusioned and disappointed that one leader could have such a significant impact.

Unfortunately, I've encountered more Sams than Neils in my career. These leaders lack authenticity and purpose in their leadership style, so their brand is perceived as mostly negative by those in their charge. The Neils are few and far between, yet they have the power to drive engagement and performance with their genuine, authentic approach to leadership. They have strong personal brands and are incredibly influential in the lives of those who are lucky enough to work with them. Neil's followers are engaged and empowered. Sam's followers are disengaged and ultimately move on to seek a better situation.

## Lack of Employee Engagement

An employee is considered 'engaged' when they care about the work they do and the company they do it for. An engaged employee will put more energy and effort into their work than they're asked or required to do.

The leadership gap is a significant cause of lagging employee engagement. The number of employees who feel their leaders inspire them to do more and be more is discouragingly low. We need more authentic leaders in the world.

Consider the following statistics:

- As few as 21 percent of employees feel motivated to do outstanding work based on how their performance is managed
- In terms of direction, only 22 percent of employees feel their leaders have a clear direction for the organization
- Only 15 percent of employees are enthusiastic about the future based on the influence of leaders in their organization
- As few as 13 percent of employees strongly agree the leadership of their organization communicates effectively[1]

Given how frequently people change jobs, it's clear they're looking for more—and in many cases, specifically from leaders. If the employee feels disconnected and demotivated, doesn't have a strong relationship with their manager, lacks clear direction or an understanding of a career path, they are at risk of leaving the organization to seek something more fulfilling.

## Generational Differences

Today's workforce is comprised of multiple generations, which makes this a challenging time for leaders. Boomers, Gen X, Gen Y, and Gen Z are all working alongside one another.

One issue related to the multi-generational workplace is the bias that some have for generations outside of their own. Boomers tend to criticize the behaviors of millennials and Gen Zers. However, boomers raised and shaped millennials and Gen Zers into young adults. The leadership perspective and expertise these older generations bring are valuable to younger generations. These generations have lived through the various stages of leader development techniques and changing workplace dynamics. Younger generations may not appreciate the wisdom and experience that boomers and Gen Xers bring to the workplace.

Accordingly, today's leaders must embrace these differences and recognize the unique contributions that each generation can bring to the workplace. Each adds value. This complexity may be one of the reasons why some of today's leaders are falling short and why so many employees are disengaged. For example, the hierarchical leadership structure that boomers grew up with simply doesn't resonate with the younger generations.

Yet, despite all these differences, leadership expectations are similar across generations. In Gallup, Inc.'s report, *How Millennials Want to Work and Live,* we find important data about the multigenerational desire to work for quality leaders: "Millennials [and members of other generations] have the same expectations of their managers: constant communication, accountability and clearly established expectations."[2]

The following chart outlines several commonly cited characteristics of each generation. Not every person will embody the characteristics of their generation, but this chart can serve as a guide to demonstrate the general differences.

| **Attributes** | **Boomers** Born between 1946 and 1964 | **Gen X** Born between 1965 and 1980 | **Gen Y** Born between 1981 and 1996 | **Gen Z** Born between 1997 – |
|---|---|---|---|---|
| **Career** | Loyal to employer | Loyal to leader | Loyal to self | Loyal to causes |
| **Values** | Ambition | Outcomes | Mentoring | Mobility and immediacy |
| **Job** | Stable career | Forward-thinking opportunities | Meaningful work that fulfills ambition | Work that allows them to live their purpose and passion |

The truth is, we all have a lot to learn from each generation. If we can approach the workplace with open minds and open hearts, we will benefit from the diversity of today's workforce.

I believe we can find a multigenerational common ground. The unifying element is authentic leadership. Each generation embodies deep loyalties, unique but complementary values, and an ability to drive professional success through expectations and ambitions. Good, authentic leaders can align their team members' complementary values toward common goals. Conversely, poor leaders can exaggerate the problems and drive even more of a divide between employees.

## We Need More Personal in Business

One of my favorite movies is *You've Got Mail*, starring Tom Hanks and Meg Ryan. A powerful scene strikes me each time I watch it. After the giant retailer Fox Books puts a tiny second-generation bookshop out of business, Joe Fox (Tom Hanks) tells Kathleen Kelly (Meg Ryan), the former shop owner, "It was business. It wasn't personal." Kathleen replies, "That just means it wasn't personal to *you*. What's so wrong with being personal anyway?"

Kathleen Kelly was right on target by saying that everything should be personal. In today's business environment, customers have come to expect personalized messages, relevant content, and curated lists based on likes and past purchases. A strong and lasting business relationship isn't just transactional. It's personal.

Consumers expect more, demand better service, and require that businesses *know them*. And guess what? So do employees. Regardless of generational label, we all desire meaningful experiences and relationships with our leaders. So, as leaders, we need to know who our employees are and understand what motivates them.

I once worked with an executive leader who'd been told by the CEO that he needed to work with a coach to improve his interactions with employees. To his credit, he shared this with his staff. However, I'm not sure he fully embraced the coaching process or the lessons. Without a greeting, he'd burst into my office and fire questions at me about our marketing plans. Often, he'd kick out whoever was in my office at the time or demand that I end a call so he could launch into his line of questioning. Then, as he was leaving my office, he'd seemingly recall the coach's lessons and ask, "So, how's the family?"

Leaders who behave in a transactional way may not recognize the consequences of their behavior. The demands of the business and the busyness of their days can cause them to neglect to deliver what their followers need from them. Employees need to know and feel that they're part of something greater than themselves. They need to understand that they play an important role in the organization's success. They need to know that their leaders respect and appreciate their contribution. Leaders also need to recognize the commitment employees make to the business; it's where they apply their talents and spend most of their time away from families and other activities. The transactional aspects of a job should be the paycheck and the benefits.

Disingenuous efforts won't work. Some of the most authentic leaders I've worked with make time for a simple smile and hello when passing employees in the hall. They stop by employees' desks and introduce themselves and ask what they're working on. Some ask about a family member who's ill, or how a child's football team is doing. One leader I worked with would come into the lunchroom and sit at different tables each day to interact with employees. The little things really matter.

The point is, the leader must be authentic in their approach—otherwise it won't be seen as sincere.

## Leadership and Company Culture

Business culture is a culmination of the beliefs and behaviors of leaders and employees. It develops organically. To create a strong culture, a company's leaders must align with the company's purpose, especially as more people are seeking meaningful work. A company's founders and leaders define its purpose and may or may not embody it consistently.

Authentic leaders whose values are aligned with the company's values and purpose create a strong company culture. They're clear about what matters to them, and it's in sync with what matters to the company. It's easy to spot when a leader's values match those of the company. The employees are clear about their roles and understand how their efforts contribute to the overall company purpose. The leader ensures that the employees feel that connection and, as a result, their employees believe in them. They are inspired and engaged.

Many leaders fall short when it comes to conveying and embodying values, for various reasons. Ultimately, if the leader isn't clear about what matters to them personally and professionally, they won't be able to provide the most authentic and effective leadership. Employees want to feel that their work matters to the organization and that it aligns with the company's values. Unfortunately, less than a quarter of all employees in the U.S. actually feel this way.[3]

Culture matters. And regardless of the values stated in the company handbook, leaders define it. In my career, I've seen firsthand the true impact that leaders have on a culture. I've worked for organizations where employees were encouraged and empowered in a *be one team* culture. I've also experienced a *comply or die* culture.

In the *be one team* cultures, the CEOs consistently conveyed the company's purpose. The executive leaders were in sync and supported and respected each other. The leaders at all levels understood their roles and the rules of engagement with employees and customers. The employees knew where the company was going and could both articulate and deliver on the brand promise. The company values meant something—they created a sense of pride and camaraderie. The culture was consistently embodied by all levels of leadership and there was a ripple effect across the entire organization. Employees were engaged and aligned, meaning there was no leadership gap and people spoke and behaved with authenticity. Customer experiences were a direct reflection of the culture: positive. What mattered was clear, leaders were authentic, and the energy was palpable.

My experience in the *comply or die* culture was dramatically different. The CEO led by fear, micromanaged employees, and encouraged competition among executive leaders. The company purpose was constantly changing. It was nonnegotiable and always a reaction to the latest opportunity or threat. The executive leaders were forced to comply and deliver the changing messages to employees. This style of leadership directly and indirectly conveyed uncertainty and angst about the company's future. Values existed only in the handbook. But the external message delivered to customers was one of collaboration, camaraderie, and high performance. Some employees felt that the face presented to customers was a joke, as the actual experiences they were having were significantly different. An employee survey revealed many inconsistencies. The leaders reviewed the survey but felt they knew better, so little changed. Although the culture was intense and fast-paced, employee energy and engagement were low. Clocking out at five o'clock on the dot was the norm. The leaders were baffled as to why. They shouldn't have been.

## Your Brain at Work

Modeling is a form of survival. The reptilian and limbic parts of the brain learn and repeat behaviors in order to keep us safe—to help us be like others in our environment. Modeling behavior also creates a primitive sense of belonging when there's a perceived threat in the environment.

Most of us will never face the life-threatening dangers that early humans did, but the stress we feel in our daily lives is very real. In fact, repeated stress keeps us in fight-or-flight mode. If we're dealing with a challenging boss or a toxic culture, our brains work overtime to help us survive and belong.

The neocortex is the most evolved part of our brain. When our neocortex is activated, we can think clearly and weigh options. When we use the neocortex, we thrive. We're no longer worried about survival, safety, or belonging. We can focus on innovation and contribution. We can think of ways to approach a situation and weigh pros and cons without the threat of danger. When a company's culture is strong and positive and its leaders are authentic, employees feel a sense of belonging and can activate the most powerful part of their brains.

## Fear and the Thinking Brain

Obviously, we'd all prefer to be in situations where we can actively use our thinking brain. Unfortunately, many people fear things in their work environments: a leader, a peer, getting fired, underperforming, or not fitting in. When we're afraid, our reptilian and limbic brains are more active than our neocortex. You've probably been there—in a situation where you felt your brain wasn't working properly. You froze, couldn't think of a response, cowered, or avoided a person or situation to remain safe. It was debilitating.

Leaders have the power to drive people into fight-or-flight mode or to empower them to have full access to their brains and contribute at a high level. Powerful leaders generate a ripple effect. Authentic leaders create a positive ripple that energizes many people. Leaders focused on power create a negative ripple that can drown efforts and weaken engagement.

## Negative Experiences

Negative experiences are often a result of ineffective leaders, which you may recognize from these traits.

See if you can identify which of these negative traits apply in each of the following stories. They're from real people who shared their experiences regarding negative leadership in a survey I conducted amongst millennials and Gen Xers.

Erin

*"Shawn was one of the most passive-aggressive leaders I'd ever met. He made you question or second-guess his responses, which led to needless conversations that created frustration. He was often condescending, and his direction was unclear. I watched myself and the rest of the creative team grow increasingly frustrated by his lack of leadership experience. Shawn lacked the ability to clearly communicate with or build confidence in his team."*

Amy

*"When I was an occupational therapy student, my supervisor*

*was impatient and used intimidation tactics and trick questions throughout my internship. These affected me emotionally. I suppose he felt as if he were making me tougher, but it simply resulted in daily anxiety about work. I had to keep pushing myself to do my best and get through each day in order to get the credit. His management style made him unapproachable."*

Kate

*"Despite my hard work and dedication, one of my bosses (when I was an intern) always seemed really annoyed with me. He never communicated realistic expectations. He was demeaning, and I never felt like I was helpful or intelligent. As a leader, he didn't inspire me to enjoy my work or make me feel valued."*

Sal

*"I was assigned to a project and teamed with a colleague and senior leader whom I'm convinced wanted my colleague to fail. From the beginning, I was concerned because the team lacked the expertise to achieve success. The leader knew this, and it felt like a disingenuous game. I'd hoped to learn from his experience, but unfortunately that wasn't the result. We did a lot of work without clear direction. The leader would just take whatever we did and, two days before the deadline, create his own presentation disregarding all our work and not explaining why he changed things. We never had the opportunity to learn and grow from his experience and wisdom."*

Elizabeth

*"My new boss, a young leader who was put in an important position before he was ready, was impatient, dishonest, and feared. You never knew what kind of meeting you were going to have with him. Was he having a good day or a bad day? Had someone told him something he believed was your fault?*

*I left most meetings feeling like I was going to vomit. He'd often tell me to do something and then weeks later be confrontational and upset that I was doing the thing he'd told me to do. He would nitpick about the most meaningless things to prove a point. I think he focused on little things because he was in a role he didn't understand, and it was how he kept control."*

TODD

*"I had a leader I liked, but over time it became painfully clear that she was doing dishonest things that were harmful to my team and me. When I worked overtime on a project that saved the company hundreds of thousands of dollars in production costs, I learned that my manager had taken credit for the project's success. Soon I realized she was taking credit for a lot of my work while her boss counseled me for not carrying my weight. My team began modeling this bad practice and the environment became toxic. It was one of the longest and most stressful years of my life and sadly impacted me at work and at home."*

Each of these experiences had a lasting impact on the individual. The leadership styles and tactics varied, but they all resulted in negative emotions and disengagement.

You can probably relate to some of these examples of both good and bad leaders. Maybe you even recognize some of the behaviors in yourself. These kinds of cringeworthy behaviors stick with us, shape us, and teach us. We learn what to do and what *not* to do based on how leaders make us feel.

*You* can help fill the leadership gap. Unfortunately, the gap is widening. Employee engagement is suffering. Many cultures aren't driven by clear values that employees can rally behind. The world needs authentic leaders.

Let's revisit the key takeaways from Chapter 1, *Authentic Leadership*:

- Leaders aren't made by status or title

- Authentic leadership starts with a deep connection to what matters
- Authentic leaders create a positive ripple effect

In Chapter 2, *Determine What Matters*, you'll explore what matters to you and how various people and experiences have helped to shape that.

# Chapter 2
# Determine What Matters

> *Watch your thoughts, they become your words. Watch your words, they become your actions. Watch your actions, they become your habits. Watch your habits, they become your character. Watch your character, it becomes your destiny.*
>
> Ralph Waldo Emerson

When people become clear about what matters to them and leverage their unique strengths, they ignite their leadership power. They become their best selves and are consistent in their words and actions. When this happens, anything is possible. Leaders emerge.

The definition of *what matters* in the context of this book and the process you're about to embark on is this: *the people and things in your life that are most important to you and bring you the greatest joy personally and professionally*. Discovering *what matters* to you means exploring your early life and influences, who you are, what's most important to you, the things that motivate you, and the goals you're striving for.

In this chapter, you will learn:

- How your experiences have shaped the leader you are today
- That your successes and setbacks will test your leadership
- What will motivate you to achieve your goals

You'll find questions posed throughout this chapter. Visit www.danelipartners.com/books/justdoyou to get your companion workbook to capture your responses.

The process of uncovering what matters to you begins with metacognitive practices that have helped people become extraordinarily clear about what it takes to be an authentic leader. Simply put, metacognition is *an awareness and understanding of one's thought processes and an appreciation of what one knows.* In Daneli Partners' leadership discovery process[1], you'll reflect on experiences and people who have impacted you.

Why is this important? Your leadership expectations and point of view come from the experiences that had the most profound effect on you, including those from the best leaders in your life, and accompanied by your own definition of success. You'll seek to recreate patterns of positive experiences when you start a new job. When you aren't able to recreate these positive patterns, you'll become discontented and disengaged. Knowing, in advance, where the foundations of your positive experiences are will enable you to identify the ingredients in each job or situation that you can tap into to recreate the experiences you seek.

You will also seek to avoid negative patterns and leaders from your past. You will look to solve those issues, unconsciously or consciously, in your actions. You'll have to make choices about how you'll react in these negative situations. Will you become the leader you wish you had regardless of the examples around you?

Identifying what matters is a prerequisite to leading with purpose, authenticity, and influence. You'll dive deeply into your past, explore the present, and dream of the future. I'll share stories from people who describe what matters to them, and I'll challenge you to think about the same questions.

Working through this chapter may take some time, and I encourage you to do so at your own pace. Then, come back to it and review your responses to make sure you feel you've answered the questions honestly and from the heart. This is important, as your responses will be referenced in later chapters as you begin to define your personal brand.

## Focus Area: Early Life and Leader Influencers

The experiences you had while growing up and as a young adult had a profound impact on who you are. You may have strong feelings about something without really thinking about why. The *why* has been shaped by those who've influenced you and the valuable life lessons you've learned from both positive and negative experiences. Reflecting on these experiences and exploring why they stand out in your mind will give you many insights about yourself. You'll also gain valuable insights about what leadership means to you personally.

As you explore your past and think about the experiences that had the biggest impact on you, you'll see that the people at the center played a critical leadership role in your life.

Think about the individuals in your family who deeply influenced you in your youth. Who are they? Perhaps these leadership influencers spent time with you and nurtured you. Maybe they challenged you and pushed you to do more and become more. Or, if you had a quiet leader in your family, as I did (my grandfather), perhaps you benefited from their leading by example and their sharing poignant words of wisdom at key moments.

My grandfather, whom I introduced earlier, had a powerful impact on me even though he was only in my life until I was ten. He was a man of few words, and he chose them carefully. I felt I could accomplish anything when I was around him. He was the first person to instill the belief in me that I could do anything I put my mind to. My grandfather planted this seed and I owe my tenacity to him and his faith in me.

As I look back and appreciate my grandfather and how he made me feel, I realize he influenced what I expect of leaders —and I carried these expectations into my adult life. Bill and Neil had leadership styles that resonated with me because, like my grandfather, they pushed me to be my best and they believed in me. I thrived and grew as a leader when I worked with them.

## Related Stories

CJ

*"It always comes back to my dad. I was fortunate enough to have him coach me for many years in youth sports and teach me valuable life lessons on and off the field. I believe that the time I spent with him that revolved around sports is what has shaped my character and how I approach life every day. I recently encountered probably the hardest decision I'll ever have to make, and I realized afterward that his approval and acknowledgment of how proud he was of me and my decision meant more to me than anyone else's. I strive to be successful like him, day in and day out."*

Alyssa

*"My dad has been the most influential person in my life. I'm thirty-two years old and I lost him to cancer when I was twenty-three. My dad worked his way up from science teacher to principal to superintendent to district superintendent. He was still working when he passed away. I always knew he was a great boss and leader from the way teachers would talk about him. He was a true professional. My dad always remained calm and had a great sense of humor even when he was stressed-out. He always had a solution for everything and treated all his employees with the same respect."*

## Your Familial Leader Influencers

Take a moment to think about this question and record your response in your companion workbook.

Who in your family had significant influence on you in your youth?

Describe these people.

Why were they important to you and your development?

## Other Leader Influencers

Now think about leader influencers outside your family, such as teachers, professors, coaches, religious leaders, or friends. Who are they? Why were they important to your development? You may have benefited from many positive experiences with leaders in school or college, but it's likely that one person in particular comes to mind because something they did changed you in a positive way. Maybe they opened up your mind. Maybe you pushed yourself to do your best in order to impress this leader. If you're thinking of a friend, you may be recalling a time when they helped you overcome something difficult or supported you in a meaningful way.

Tommy and I met at Dick's Sporting Goods in 1988 and have been friends ever since. Tommy's positive attitude and energy was infectious. We were both young and at the beginning of our careers. When my stress level would rise, Tommy always had a joke or funny story to break the tension. Although he was stressed out too, he'd offer help whenever he could. Tommy was a trusted peer and confidant. We grew up together and found our way as leaders in a fast-paced company.

As each new leadership challenge came our way, we both had to scale to meet the requirements of our roles. Tommy was important to my professional development because he offered a different perspective, and he sought me out for my perspective as well. We could work through things together, and I trusted him completely. We shared common values and wanted to do the best we could for the company.

My experience with Tommy helped set the bar for professional peer/leader relationships. After I left Dick's, I sought to recreate that kind of trusting camaraderie. Fortunately, I've had other peer-leader relationships like the one I had with Tommy. I feel fortunate to have experienced it early on and to have been able to carry this leadership example into my other work experiences.

## Related Stories

JENNA

*"My high school guidance counselor, Jamie, was caring, as many counselors are, but he was also invested in the students. He took the time to get to know us personally—who our families were, our hobbies and passions. As I was looking at colleges, Jamie encouraged me to pursue the social sciences (sociology, psychology, etc.) as he felt they would be a natural fit with my personality. He helped me identify and understand my strengths. He built my confidence, inspired me, and assisted me as I navigated the lists of potential educational and career paths. I'm fortunate to have had Jamie as my mentor as I was entering the career stage of my life. Without his guidance, I may have chosen a different field of study that I wouldn't have felt nearly as passionate about."*

NICOLE

*"In high school, I had a swim coach many would call 'hard core.' It seemed as if we were put through intense workouts, under strict rules, and yelled at daily. However, I always knew it wasn't to punish us but to make us better athletes and people. I could tell he was trying to push us to become*

*better versions of ourselves and show us that no matter how hard something is, you can find the strength if you put in the work. My coach always seemed to know how much further to push without discouraging us. I believe having this 'keep pushing forward' mind-set drilled into me at a young age has helped me in other areas of my life. No matter what kind of situation I come across, I always find a solution. When it seems like no matter what I do and the problem is still there, I keep going. I have to thank my coach for pushing me into believing that I could always improve."*

ANDREW

*"I didn't think much of musical theater when I went into the class. I thought it would be a minimal amount of work that involved watching old musicals, and that it was probably going to be taught by a monotone professor. It was so much more than that. My musical theater and acting professor, Jim, was passionate about musical theater. I became a believer in what he was teaching and found that I enjoyed musical theater. He was so positive and easy to approach. I think his positivity and his attitude toward the topic really influenced me to appreciate different things and to step out of my comfort zone."*

## Your Other Leader Influencers

Take a moment to think about this question and record your responses in your companion workbook.

Who are the people who influenced you deeply in your life? They might be friends, teachers, religious leaders, professors, or coaches.

Describe these people.

Why were they important to you and your development?

## Profound Positive Experiences

Often, leaders we encounter create a positive experience, and perhaps they even make us think differently about ourselves as a result.

As you explore your past and think about the experiences that had the biggest impact on you, you'll recall times when your feelings were positive, when you increased your knowledge and felt joy and exhilaration. Times when your confidence blossomed, and the lessons were easy to grasp. At these times, your neocortex was learning and working at a high level. You felt smart and alive. You felt nurtured and safe. You felt as if you belonged. These experiences could have happened in any context: academic, business, or otherwise. Leaders played an important role in these experiences because they helped to create the safe environment in which you were able to thrive. As you reflect on your positive experiences, ask yourself, "What did I learn?"

Several years ago, I felt drawn to help people in my community and decided to offer my help by training to be a Stephen Minister. Stephen Ministries is an organization that represents more than 170 denominations of Christianity and extends the efforts of the church into communities by training laypersons to provide one-on-one care for those who request support. Students of the program gain insights into the thoughts and feelings of those hurting and develop relational and caring skills that can be applied to all aspects of life.

It was a lot for me to take on at that stage of my life. I had two young children and a demanding job. Having no prior training for this ministry, I was also a bit intimidated. But Irene, the leader of the Stephen Ministries program, welcomed me with open arms.

The training program was twenty weeks long. Irene's leadership style immediately created a nurturing environment in which all of us could learn and grow. She made us feel as if we could change the world one person at a time. I felt alive and easily grasped the content. Although there was a great deal to learn, it all clicked into place and felt natural. The training experience and the experiences caring for people as a Stephen Minister were some of the most rewarding of my life. So much of what I learned as a Stephen Minister has been applied to all aspects of my personal and professional life. Irene's leadership had a significant and positive effect on me.

## Related Stories

Erin

*"This leader was one of a few female executives in a male-dominated world, and I looked up to her right away for several reasons. She had grace under pressure. She was poised, professional, and a savvy business leader. And she was one of the most intelligent people I'd ever met. Upon accepting the position, I didn't report directly to her, but after a few years of proving myself, she gave me a chance to take my career to the next level. It was her decision that led me to the career path I'm on today—one I couldn't have possibly imagined just a few years ago. And for that I am grateful. Years later, I find myself reflecting on her leadership style and using what I learned to lead my own team."*

Todd

*"As someone with a bachelor's degree in art, I don't fit the core expectations of a leader in business. I landed a part-time job that utilized my Photoshop skills. The job was straightforward, but it evolved beyond anything I could have imagined. With my leader's guidance, it wasn't long before I*

*was involved in large projects that would impact our entire department. Every project seemed to be an evolution of a previous process, and my peers and I had every opportunity to jump into the mix with directors and VPs alike. I was soon sitting in on the weekly director meetings, discussing upcoming projects for the year, and was tasked with some big responsibilities and a lot of trust to see projects through. I stretched every single skill I had and gained many new skills. My leader never told me that I wasn't capable of something. If there was a project beyond my experience, she would find a way for me grow, improve myself, and learn over time. I felt a bigger return on my hard work and dedication because of the doors that those experiences and education opened. In that environment, the workplace felt more like a home than a business. I and many others in the department owe that to our fearless leader."*

## Your Profound Positive Experiences

Take a moment to think about these questions and record your response in your companion workbook.

Were there specific experiences with leaders in your life that affected you in a positive way? A way that caused you to think differently about yourself?

List three to five words that describe these leaders.

What have you carried forward from your experiences with these leaders?

What behaviors have evolved as a result of those experiences?

## Profound Negative Experiences

It may not be as easy to see the lessons in the bad experiences. While you were in them, you might have felt trapped. It's likely that your reptilian and limbic brains were working overtime during that difficult period in your life. This kept you in survival mode and limited your ability to access your neocortex in order to weigh options to work creatively and strategically. When you're in high-stress survival mode, it's difficult to learn and grow. You need to remove yourself from the situation before you can reflect and process the experience. Often, you can pull valuable life lessons from negative experiences if you view them from a fresh perspective after the fact. As you reflect on your negative experiences, ask yourself, "What did I learn?"

I had a negative experience with a peer at one point in my career that deeply affected me. Up until that point, I'd had mostly positive peer/leader relationships in each organization I'd worked in. Don't get me wrong—it wasn't all sunshine and roses. Disagreements occurred and challenges with others needed to be worked through. But until I worked with Jason, I didn't realize just how much another leader could affect me personally. Jason had been with the company since college. He was in his late forties and well-established in his role when we started working together. And I brought with me certain expectations and a desire to create a strong collaborative peer relationship.

While I was on the learning curve, getting to know the business, Jason appeared to be supportive. Privately, he was working behind the scenes with other colleagues to undermine me. When I realized this was happening, my reptilian and limbic brains kicked into high gear, and I started focusing on the threats around me. I became paranoid about who might be believing what Jason was saying. I was fearful that I would lose my job and felt as if I weren't performing at the highest level. I couldn't think straight.

If you'd asked me back when I was in the middle of that situation, I wouldn't have been able to draw a lesson from the experience. In hindsight, I realize that the experience with Jason helped me to see what's possible in a toxic work environment and what one bad leader is capable of. The ripple effect on me and others was powerful. As difficult as that situation was at the time, I know it has made me a better leader and coach. I can relate to my clients and better empathize with their circumstances when a toxic leader is affecting them.

## Related Stories

JOE

*"My micromanager supervisor couldn't properly delegate work. He'd interfere or change how I was working, and it made me feel as though he didn't trust me or that I couldn't do adequate work. I've learned that it's important as a leader to trust your staff, and although it can be beneficial to be involved in their tasks and provide input, being too involved and checking in constantly and changing how they do things can negatively impact the staff long term."*

JONATHAN

*"After a new promotion, I was working with the CFO on inventory levels and reducing operational costs. This particular CFO was the kind who sat behind a desk and worked solely off numbers (not what was on the floor physically). I would ask for her help and the only answer I'd get was, "Can't you figure this out? I don't have time." Soon I was avoiding her. She was intelligent and knowledgeable but lacked the understanding and patience to help someone new. I wanted someone who could show me the ropes, help me develop a plan to reduce inventory, and work with me as a team. Months later I decided I needed to make a change. I started to read. I read all about LEAN manufacturing, inventory turns, buyer guides, and how to lean out your inventory without running out of parts. I found out quickly that if you take control of a situation, you can control your destiny. She wasn't a good leader, but if it hadn't been for*

*her, I would never have challenged myself and stepped up in a situation I was unfamiliar with. "*

## Your Negative Experiences

Take a moment to think about how to answer these questions and record your responses in your companion workbook.

Were there specific experiences with leaders in your life that affected you in a very negative way? A way that caused you to think differently about yourself?

List three to five words that describe these leaders.

What have you carried forward from your experiences with these leaders?

What behaviors have evolved as a result of those experiences?

## Defining Moments

There have likely been times in your life when you've been asked or had the opportunity to step up and lead. These are your defining moments.

Think about something you consider to be a great accomplishment in your life. How did you feel when you accomplished it? What did you learn about yourself? Stepping into the unknown can be daunting but also incredibly rewarding. You might have been trying to rely on your reptilian and limbic brains to keep you in a safe place, but the situation was pushing you outside your comfort zone and challenging you to apply the power of your neocortex!

One of my defining moments occurred in 1994, when Dick's Sporting Goods's CEO Ed Stack announced that he was relocating the corporate office from Binghamton, New York, to Pittsburgh, Pennsylvania. I was director of advertising and had a team of ten people reporting to me. My husband also worked for the company, so we quickly agreed to relocate. Next, I needed to communicate the plans to my team and determine who would be relocating. I also needed to interview replacements (in Pittsburgh) for those employees who decided not to relocate. The idea of moving my department, transitioning to a new city, and training new employees was overwhelming. We had an aggressive advertising schedule and couldn't miss a beat. I had to step up and lead the team through the transition.

What made this even more challenging was that I was pregnant with my son, Andrew. My due date was two weeks before we had to report to the new office in Pittsburgh. I had to ensure that my team was in place, all the necessary equipment was moved and set up in Pittsburgh, and hit all the deadlines for the newspaper advertising. Plus, my husband and I needed to sell our house, find a house in Pittsburgh, and register our young daughter for first grade. Oh, and I needed to deliver my son on time. No pressure! It was one of the most challenging and stressful periods in my life.

Fortunately, most of my team relocated to Pittsburgh and those who elected to stay in the Binghamton area found new jobs elsewhere with our help and support. We successfully integrated the new hires into the team. The equipment arrived and was set up so we didn't miss a deadline. My planning and attention to detail paid off! My son was born four days early, and we made the trip to Pittsburgh as a family when he was two weeks old. I look back on that time with great pride and a sense of accomplishment. Absolutely every aspect of my life changed all at once. Reflecting on that time makes me feel confident that I can handle what comes my way. Other moves and life changes have seemed minimal in comparison.

## Related Stories

AMY

*"When my boss went on extended leave, I took over her role as rehab director. This was challenging, and both our company and treatment site went through many changes. I had several*

*ups and downs, and the role was very stressful at times. In spite of this, I always tried to remain positive and do my best for my staff and patients. I learned the importance of communication, helping therapists build on their strengths, and working together as a team with respect for one another. I learned valuable techniques for managing a variety of personalities and motivating them to do their best for their patients each day."*

Kourtney

*"While in college, I had a job that initially had four supervisors but quickly dropped down to two. I was sharing the head-supervisor position with another employee, but then he was demoted. While this didn't mean a huge change for me, soon after, the scheduling supervisor was let go for stealing from an employee. As a result of his termination, I stepped forward to assist the payroll supervisor with scheduling. This was overwhelming because I was not trained to do payroll. I had to teach myself the system, and I had twenty-nine schedules to manage. I had to work hard to make the schedule flawless. While this was challenging at first, it spoke volumes to my boss about my character, abilities, and dependability. The whole situation ended up being very rewarding for me."*

## Your Defining Moments

Think about a defining moment/great accomplishment in your life when you had to step up and lead.

How did you feel?

What did you learn about yourself?

## Setbacks

Setbacks happen to everyone. You've undoubtedly experienced something in your lifetime that you'd go back and change if you could. With the wisdom of hindsight, you can see the situation differently now. Maybe you now possess the skills or knowledge to handle the situation better than you could before. It's important to spend time reflecting on these situations, as uncomfortable as doing so may be, because they give you insights into the kind of leader you wish you'd been in that moment. The fact that you can see the missed leadership opportunity now indicates that you have what it takes to create positive experiences going forward.

As a young leader, the most challenging situation I faced was having to fire an employee. This is never easy to do, and frankly, I'd hoped I'd never have to. But as a leader, that hope is unrealistic. Shannon was a member of my team and had been with the company for about a year. When she started, she was a great performer and helped me immensely on several projects. She was eager to learn and offered to help wherever she was needed. I felt she had great potential with the company. But then Shannon began calling in sick each week. Sometimes she wouldn't show up and would call a few hours after her required start time to let me know she wasn't going to make it in that day. I sought advice from my leader and from human resources. Shannon had exceeded her allotted sick time, and I was told to counsel her and write her up.

I did as I'd been instructed. I conducted the discussion and handed her the written warning. Shannon was a bit shocked, yet she didn't offer any explanation for her frequent absences, nor did I seek to understand what this explanation might be. Unfortunately, the situation didn't change, so I had to call Shannon into my office and fire her a few weeks later. To this day, I regret how that conversation went. As it was my first termination, I was professional and followed the guidelines from human resources. But upon reflection, I wish I'd given Shannon the opportunity to talk about what was happening in her life and why she was missing so much work. She might have elected not to share this information, but I could have been more confident in my leadership abilities and should have relied less on the black-and-white employee manual. I learned a valuable lesson through that failure. I should have reached out when the behavior began instead of waiting until it escalated to a termination-worthy offense. Things might have turned out more positively. I'll never know. What I do know is that I've handled all my relationships with my employees differently since then.

## Related Stories

Keegan

*"My fiancée and I started a business with a close friend. We felt we knew him well and had always had a positive relationship with him, so we expected the same in our business. As the business grew, we moved out of state, far from the support of family and friends. We rented a home together and worked on the business day and night—well, my fiancée and I did! We saw a different side of our friend when we lived and worked with him. He had a terrible temper and poor work ethic. While we rushed around filling orders, he was off doing other things like going to the gym and working on hobbies. We became frustrated, angry, and disappointed that he wasn't the person we'd always known him to be. I confronted him several times, but it always led to an argument. He just wasn't as motivated to drive the business as we were. We ended up parting ways and lost a business partner and a friend. It was a setback for sure, but we got back on our feet and ended up building a stronger business after that experience. We learned that we needed to maintain a positive atmosphere and work ethic in our business. We didn't have the time or energy to manage someone else's negativity. When we bring people into our business now, we're careful to find the right fit."*

Rachel

*"In my previous role at a major manufacturer, I was asked to*

*develop and lead design-thinking training globally. Since I was only three years into my career, I didn't feel prepared for the role. I also wasn't supported by a strong leader. However, I took the challenge, determined to do my best and build on the momentum our team had been building over the past few years. The experience was both rewarding and dispiriting. Having the opportunity to build something new, see it through, and adopt it was an extremely valuable way to see the impact of my work, as well as learn from it. At the same time, it helped me realize that this wasn't what I wanted to spend the rest of my life doing. I'd given my whole self to this project for half a year, and while I learned a great deal through the process, met some incredible people, and honed skills, it left me feeling empty rather than excited. I felt I'd failed in some way. Ultimately, this setback was important as it helped me decide on my next step, which meant chalking up the successes and failures from this experience and moving on."*

## Your Setbacks

Think about a setback/defining moment in your life when you felt as if you failed or didn't lead effectively.

How did you feel?

What did you learn about yourself?

## Inspirational Influencers

The life lessons and leaders in your past have taught you a great deal and helped shape who you are today. You already have a picture in your head about who has impacted you the most. You already know which stories and which leaders stand out in your mind. You already know what leadership looks like to you based on your life experiences.

Now, consider who in your life has inspired you to dream more, learn more, do more, or become more. This special person has made you want to be a better person because of the kind of person they are. They have, through their actions, caused you to push yourself and to aspire to have the kind of impact they have on the world.

For me, this person is my father. Through his actions, my father has always inspired me to become more in both my personal and professional life. As a young child, I watched my father work hard. He went to work every day at IBM and then came home and always seemed to have a project going on around the house. Everywhere we went, people knew my dad and liked him. I remember thinking how much I wanted to be like him. And I wanted to be liked as much as he was.

In his personal life, my dad is a caregiver. His parents divorced when he was a teen and he helped care for his mother and younger sister. Later in life, when his parents were ill, he took care of them while managing his job and his own family. I never heard my dad complain, even when he was clearly exhausted. Caring for others is part of who he is. His most important caregiver role came when my mother became ill. My father took over everything around the house, including the cooking, which he learned how to do. He helped my mother navigate her debilitating disease and assisted her through each increasingly difficult phase. He managed her medications and made sure she followed the doctor's instructions. The example he set for his family was incredible. I can only hope to be half the caregiver he's been if faced with that challenge.

## Related Stories

### CJ

*"My mother has always inspired me with her kindness toward others and her belief that everyone should be treated the same. She has always been there to help, guide, and support me in*

*anything I do in life. She pushes me to become the best person I can be. She once told me, "People won't remember the things you did, but they'll always remember the way YOU made them feel."*

Jenna

*"This is an easy one—my little sister, Sara. Sara is bold, outgoing, adventurous, and independent. Growing up, she seemed to always know exactly what she wanted and wouldn't let anything stand in her way. Sara is passionate about everything she does. She holds on to what she truly believes in. Having the ability to watch her navigate life so courageously has been an inspiration to dream more, learn more, do more, and become more."*

Nicole

*"Someone who has inspired me to dream more and do more is my fiancé. From the beginning, he inspired me to become better in all aspects of life, from pushing me in the gym to starting multiple businesses. When I thought I'd end up stuck in a job I had no passion for, he said, 'Let's start a business instead.' When I didn't believe that I could be an entrepreneur, he showed me that anyone can be a business owner if they believe in what they're doing and put in the work. Now we motivate each other, help each other, and grow together."*

Sal

*"My uncle Mark, a dentist who owns his own practice, worked long hours and had patient emergencies on the weekend yet always found time to teach me and his son James. Mark would often take us to Barnes & Noble and encourage us to read things that interested us. From a young age, I started spending most of my time in the business section. Those trips with Uncle Mark and my cousin helped me learn more and develop my business mind. The thing I learned most from him is the power of*

*time. Leaders spend time with their people. Mark always made time for me, regardless of how busy life got, and he was always fully present and participating. I wanted to become more because of Mark."*

Sara

*"I aspired to learn from my VP when I was in a director role. What's always inspired me is her demeanor and how she treats me. She's always kind, chooses the right words and tone, and she truly believes in me. And while she pushes me to do what I believe is right, she's also subtly directive. Whether she pushes me to grow or I grow because I want to work with her, I want to impress her—I want to deliver a great project. I truly appreciate how she has made me feel about myself and my work. I want my team to feel that way about themselves too.*

## Your Inspirational Influencers

Who has inspired you to dream more, learn more, do more, and become more?

## Focus Area: Self-Awareness

Now that you've had a chance to revisit your past and reflect on the experiences and people who had the biggest impact on you, let's turn the lens inward. As you begin to think about how *you do you*, you'll need to dig deeper into what drives you and how you see yourself.

When was the last time you paused to ask yourself, "Who am I?" Consider the words you'd use to describe yourself to others. You might say something like, "I'm driven and ambitious," or maybe, "I'm a bit introverted and introspective." Now consider the words that friends, family members, and coworkers might use to describe you.

This will give you a picture of yourself based on your own perspective as well as the perspectives of others in your life.

Who are you?

What words would you use to describe yourself?

What words would your family and friends use to describe you?

What words would your coworkers use to describe you?

You may have a lot of people in your world: family, friends, colleagues, your professional network, your social media connections, neighbors, acquaintances, etc. It's important to identify who really matters most to you. That's not to suggest that some people aren't important and worthy of your time and attention. Rather, it's meant to clarify those people in your life who you feel *most* strongly about—the people you are committed to.

Who matters to you in your personal life?

Who matters to you in your professional life?

Another piece of your identity is defined by the work you've chosen to do. Often, one of the first questions that comes up when meeting someone new is "What do you do?" or "What are you studying?" Think about whether your field of choice is fulfilling. Does it make you feel as if you're working toward something meaningful? Finding meaning in your work and aligning with an organization's values is increasingly important in today's workforce, as we discussed in Chapter 1, *Authentic Leadership*.

What do you do?

What made you choose the field you're in?

Is the field what you thought it would be?

What work related to this field makes you burst with energy?

What work related to this field de-energizes you?

What work do you have to do that you don't like and would either stop doing or delegate if you could?

The things that affect you deeply—those things that really bother you as well as those commitments that are really important to you—are also key indicators of who you are.

The things that bother you could be a result of your own experiences or those of people close to you. Perhaps you want to prevent others from having the same kind of experience.

The things you commit to demonstrate what you care most about. You lose all sense of time when you're focused on these commitments—they're that important to you. These could include commitments to yourself (for example, exercising or spending time on a hobby that brings you inner fulfillment and peace).

What are the things that affect you?

What kinds of things bother you?

What commitments are important to you?

There are endless ways to express what you're committed to, what bothers you, and what matters to you.

Social media platforms allow you to tell your network exactly what you want them to know about you and what you're experiencing. An important step in the self-awareness process is to reflect on your social media presence and how accurately it represents you.

Consider how you share who you are with others.

What do you share about yourself on social media and what posts do you interact with?

Look at your social media accounts and describe your last three to five posts (consider the words, photos, or videos you chose to share).

Review the posts from others that you've liked or shared in the last week. What are they about and are there any themes that stand out to you?

## Focus Area: Career and Aspirations

You've reflected on your past and considered who you are in the present. Now, it's time to gaze upon your future.

Perhaps you're a dreamer and the future is a place where you frequently spend time—you enjoy planning and envisioning the ways you'll achieve all that you wish to. Or maybe you're a here and now kind of person who doesn't spend much time thinking about the future.

Regardless of where you are on that spectrum, to become an authentic leader, it's important to explore your motivations and aspirations in a forward-looking process.

What motivates you?

In your career, what matters to you?

What are you working toward?

Consider what you're working toward in your career. Are you the kind of person who has a five-year plan? Or do you take one step at a time and let life happen? There's no right or wrong answer, but you can likely think of a few current motivators. For instance, I often hear my clients say they want to get to the next leadership level in their company, to help others, to achieve success, wealth, and security, to learn, to be challenged—just to name a few. Those motivations may be short term or long term, depending on where the person is in their career. One client asked me if I thought that his saying *wealth* as a motivation made him sound greedy. The answer was no. He was a planner, and at thirty, he was already thinking about his goals: starting his own business before he turned fifty and funding college for his daughter. These dreams required him to plan and save accordingly. What mattered most to him at this stage was making that happen. I also work with clients whose work isn't at all aligned with their motivations and what they wish to accomplish in their lifetime. Think about where you are and what you're working toward. Are you on that path today?

What are your professional goals?

What goal would you most like to accomplish by year-end?

What job or role would you like to have in two years? Five years? Ten years?

What are your greatest barriers to success?

What are your *best bets*, the best areas in which to invest your time and energy?

At some point in your life, you likely daydreamed about winning the lottery or being in a situation where money wasn't a factor. Most of us have. This daydream allowed you to think, unencumbered by the burdens of your expenses and current responsibilities, about what you would do if you could do absolutely anything.

If you could connect your passion and your energy, what would that role look like?

What's your dream job?

When asked what they would do differently if they suddenly

became wealthy, many of my clients say they would exponentially scale what they're already doing, solve a problem that's important to them, or give back in some meaningful way. Others would completely abandon what they're doing and take on something totally different. Think about what you would do if you could connect your passion to your work and money wasn't a factor. How closely related is this to what you're doing today?

If money weren't a factor, what would you want to do for a living?

## Determine What Matters: Summary

Congratulations on your efforts thus far. Did you find this process easy, or difficult? Looking back can bring up both happy and challenging memories. Looking within can reveal some areas where you aren't your best self. Looking ahead can be daunting and feel overwhelming. But all this reflection can also be exciting and drive much-needed clarity. The most important thing to remember is that you're on a journey to live and lead with authenticity and purpose.

You've identified what matters to you as revealed through the experiences and people who helped shape you. You've started to define who you are and who's most important in your life. Your life's work, motivations, and goals are taking shape. You'll clarify all these things further as you work through the personal branding exercises later in this book.

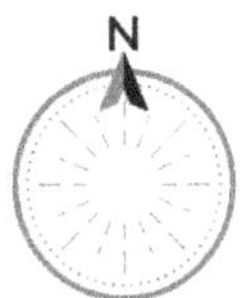


## Key Takeaways, Part One

### THE LEADER IN YOU

- The leadership gap is widening. Employee engagement and connection to company values is a growing problem. Organizations struggle to retain employees. Multigenerational workplace environments and conflicting leadership styles cause dysfunctional cultures. Employees want to be valued and to know their work has meaning

- Leadership can be confusing. Modeling the behaviors of other leaders in an effort to fit in is not the way to leadership success

- Your leadership expectations and perspectives come from your beliefs about success and positive experiences in your past. When you can't recreate that positive experience, you'll feel discontent and disengaged

- You'll also seek to avoid negative patterns from past leaders and to solve those issues in your actions. How you choose to react in negative situations dictates the leader you become, regardless of the negative examples to which you've been exposed

- The best leaders, the outliers, are authentic leaders. They are true to themselves, to their values, and to what they believe—to what matters. This is evident in the experiences they create with others. Their authenticity shines through all they do, motivates, inspires, and influences others. Authentic leaders provide encouragement and direction and are crystal clear about their role: they want to help others grow and develop. Leaders support their staff, peers, and their own leaders. They set an example

**Your leadership reflects what's inside you and how you choose to apply it.**

# Part Two

## Brands and Why They Matter

# Chapter 3
# Authentic Branding

> *About all you can do in life is be who you are. Some people will love you for you. Most will love you for what you can do for them, and some won't like you at all.*
>
> Rita Mae Brown

The concept of branding relates to both business and people. In this chapter I'll provide examples of familiar brands and explain how success is achieved when brands focus on what matters. You'll consider the attributes of people and businesses in your life and capture your point of view on the authenticity of their brands.

In this chapter, you'll learn:

- The six attributes of authentic brands
- Why a directional focus, or True North, is important

- How brand resonance and preferences affect brands
- How to rate the authenticity of a brand

Throughout my career as a marketing and branding executive, I've had the opportunity to work for and with many great brands: sporting goods brands, furniture brands, celebrity brands, and consumer packaged goods brands. In some cases, the brands were well-established and powerful, and I studied them carefully. In other cases, I helped build brands and even created some private-label brands.

Shortly after I joined Raymour & Flanigan Furniture as the senior vice president of marketing, the company was on the verge of rapid expansion into the New York metropolitan area. We needed to create a branding and marketing strategy that aligned with the true essence of the family-owned, regional furniture retailer. I applied a proven branding methodology, which included a discovery phase to understand the brand's current state and its attributes, and then developed internal and external marketing strategies based on the insights gained from this phase.

One of the special things about Raymour & Flanigan's culture was the company's recognition and celebration of employees' successes. At the end of each year, the company hosted a Celebration of Champions event. The event, held at a resort, recognized the achievements of sales associates, delivery teams, customer service associates, and others. I was responsible for developing the theme, designing all the materials, and executing the event in partnership with human resources. I loved working on the event and seeing the number of attending employees increase each year.

I sat in the audience in awe as the leading sales associates walked across the stage to receive their awards. I also had the opportunity to mingle with them and learn more about who they were, where they came from, and how they'd become so successful. What interested me the most was that each person was so different—there wasn't a common formula for *successful sales associate*. Each associate's style, sales technique, approach, and presence were as individual as they were. As I thought about this, and the fact that this successful group of sales leaders represented only a small percentage of the sales population, I wanted to learn more. I wanted to know what made them so much more successful than their peers.

I was particularly inspired by one associate whom I'll call Ravi. Ravi came to the United States as a teenager with his family. He learned English, finished high school, and went on to study business in college. After completing his degree, he held a number of sales positions prior to getting the job at Raymour & Flanigan. Ravi was deeply committed to his family and wanted to provide his children with all the educational opportunities he'd had.

When Ravi approached me at a Celebration of Champions event to thank me for helping him achieve his level of success that year, I wasn't sure what he meant. Then he shared his learning journey with me.

To improve his language skills so he could connect more deeply with his customers, Ravi studied the design magazine produced by our marketing team every month. Not only was he learning valuable design techniques to share with his customers, he was perfecting his language skills and gaining confidence. I was nearly moved to tears, amazed that the marketing efforts I'd led had affected him so personally.

After hearing more of these stories, I recognized that what set these successful sales associates apart were that they were true to themselves and their individual styles. They were clear about who they were and approached customers with confidence and conviction. Customers felt a genuine connection to them. These sales associates had personal brands that were strong and authentic. It was this realization that made me to want to create a program that would help other associates achieve this kind of leadership success through authenticity.

## Business Brands

A business brand is a product, service, retailer, or organization that has a target audience (customer or individual with a need) for whom it seeks to provide transactional and emotional value.

I've spent my career studying and developing brands to understand their essence and truths. I need to be clear on these truths from both customer and employee perspectives and present them to the world in a way that's authentic. Sometimes, things need to be corrected, developed, or improved in order for the brand to be true to itself and deliver on its promises.

Admittedly, branding and marketing often get a bad rap, and rightfully so in some cases. I don't believe in branding that masks the true nature of a product or service. I don't agree with the tactic of putting a spin on *value* in an effort to cover up flaws. This deflection tactic misleads consumers. One particularly annoying example is those pesky drug commercials that show happy people skipping about as the announcer lists the side effects. In some cases, the side effects are scarier than the original symptoms!

## Attributes of an Authentic Business Brand

When a brand is authentic, it's clear about exactly what it is and whom it serves. All of its attributes align to create experiences that drive loyalty. And a brand's authenticity drives clarity and becomes a guide for all decisions: a True North.

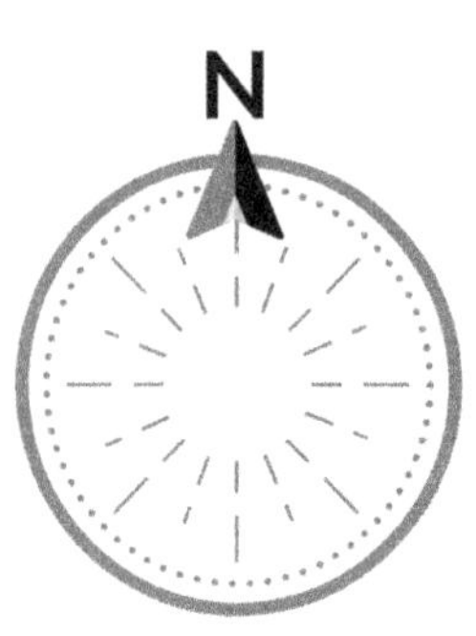


A brand's True North is a fixed point in a spinning world. One example of a brand aligned with its True North is Newman's Own. Paul Newman launched the food and beverage company in 1982. He committed to donating all profits to charitable endeavors and used some of his own recipes to create all-natural food products, vowing that quality would always trump the bottom line. This went against conventional wisdom but proved to be a recipe for success. Within the first decade of business, the company had donated $50 million.[1]

In a business world primarily focused on profit and growth, Newman's Own has a fixed directional point, a True North, that guides every decision and action.

> What could be better than to hold your hand out to people who are less fortunate than you are?
>
> Paul Newman

A business brand's authenticity can be measured by the following attributes:

- Purpose
- Promise
- Principles
- Experiences
- Presence
- Description

A brand's *purpose* is its why. The purpose defines the brand's unique offering and what it's doing for others. It's a bold statement that shares the business's reason for existing. It must be consistently evident and present what matters to the business to the world so customers and employees feel a connection with the business.

The brand *promise* is how a business tells customers what to expect—it tells them what the business commits to doing. When a business fulfills its promise, it creates loyalty. When a business breaks its promise, the brand loses credibility—employees become disengaged and customers move on. A promise is powerful.

*Principles* embody the values of the business. If employees understand and can align with the principles of the business, they'll work with passion and enthusiasm. And if customers value what a business stands for, their loyalty will be deep (and they often become the most powerful marketing tool). Many people admit they're willing to pay more for products and services if the business is aligned with a cause they believe in or has values they share.

*Experiences* are the interactions a business has with its employees and customers. They define how employees feel about working for a company and how customers feel about the brand. If the experiences are consistent and positive, both employees and customers will be loyal. If the experiences are inconsistent or negative, employees may leave and customers may select an alternative.

*Presence* is the way a brand shows up or presents itself to the world. In business, this can be in the form of logos, packaging, marketing, employee recruiting efforts, and all customer touch points (e.g., stores, the website, the products and services themselves, and customer/employee interactions). Energy and emotions are tied to a brand's presence. It's established with the intent of influencing customers to buy and enticing employees to want to work for the business. But it must be authentic in order create staying power. It can't disguise the brand's true nature.

The rubber meets the road in the brand's *description*. This is the most powerful of all the attributes. When people connect with a brand, trust it because it delivers on its promise, align with its principles, have consistent positive experiences with it, and have positive energy and emotions around it, they'll describe it with passion. And passionate people have influence with others. A brand that comes with many strong reviews attracts employees and customers. The reverse is incredibly damaging. We can all think of situations where we were let down by a business, product, service, or employer. And our voices are strong when we tell others about our undesirable experiences.

## Authenticity Rating Example

Let's consider the brand authenticity of a well-known business brand: Apple. You will have your own point of view about this brand—we'll explore brand resonance and preference later in this chapter. I'm sharing my point of view on Apple by way of example.

Here's the scoring system I've used in the following tables:

**Scoring system:**

2 This attribute is clear and delivered consistently

1 This attribute is somewhat clear and sometimes delivered

0 This attribute is unclear and not delivered

**APPLE:**

| Attributes | My point of view |
|---|---|
| **Purpose**<br>*the why of its existence* | I love Steve Jobs's mission statement for Apple (from 1980): "To make a contribution to the world by making tools for the mind that advance humankind."<br><br>**My rating: 2**. I feel Apple delivers on this consistently. |
| **Promise**<br>*what customers should expect* | "Think Different"<br><br>**My rating: 1**. Apple used to be ahead of competitors. It's still my preferred brand, but my "1" rating reflects the fact some competitors have surpassed them re: innovation. |
| **Principles**<br>*what the business values* | Innovation, quality, connectedness, user focused experiences<br><br>**My rating: 2**. Apple remains true to their principles, even without Steve Jobs. |
| **Experiences**<br>*the interactions people have with the brand* | Product usability and connectivity are generally good. If something goes wrong or I need help, I get support. I am frustrated at the timed obsolescence of my iPhone batteries, though!<br><br>**My rating: 1**. Room for improvement. |
| **Presence**<br>*how it's presented to the world* | Stylish, fresh, clean, and fashionable; high energy and exciting marketing<br><br>**My rating: 2**. Consistency over all touchpoints. |
| **Description**<br>*how I talk about the brand* | Apple devices have become part of my life socially and professionally–they are like an extension of me.<br><br>**My rating: 2**. I'm a loyal advocate. |

**Apple – Score: 10/12**

I gave the Apple brand a high score based on my experiences with the products and service. It didn't earn a perfect score based on some issues I've encountered, but I'm a satisfied, loyal customer. In my opinion, the good far outweighs the bad. I believe Apple is in alignment with its True North.

## Attributes of an Authentic Personal Brand

There are many definitions of and opinions about personal branding. And most of them focus on the professional aspect of a personal brand.

I challenge this perspective because what someone does professionally is only a slice of who the person is. A true personal brand embodies a person's essence and what makes them unique. Similar to authentic business brands, authentic personal brands clearly convey what matters. Their True North drives all decisions.

Your True North is your internal compass. It keeps you facing in the direction of what matters and who you are at the deepest level.

Martin Luther King Jr., American minister and activist, is a well-known example of a leader who created a powerful personal brand. King led the civil rights movement in the 1960s and became the most visible spokesperson for the cause. He's best known for his efforts to advance civil rights through nonviolence and civil disobedience. He said, "Darkness cannot drive out darkness; only light can do that. Hate cannot drive out hate; only love can do that." In these words, he expressed his True North.

Like that of a business brand, a personal brand's authenticity is measured by the following attributes:

- Purpose
- Promise
- Principles
- Experiences
- Presence
- Description

Your *purpose* is your why. It summarizes your gifts and defines what you want to achieve. It's a bold statement that shares your reason for being. It must be consistently delivered through your interactions with others and present what matters to you so that the people in your life can feel a deep connection with you.

Through your *promises*, you tell people what they can expect from you. You tell them how you'll commit to doing something for them. Remember, a promise is powerful. Affection and trust are built on kept promises. And a lack of these things can end personal and professional relationships.

Your *principles* embody what you value. They're developed over time and through your life experiences. These strong inner feelings about right and wrong have the power to call you to action. When you can clearly define your principles, it's easier to make decisions. The choices you make will be aligned with your values.

Your *experiences* are the interactions you have with people in your personal and professional circles, as well as with strangers. These interactions define relationships. People naturally gravitate toward people who provide consistent and positive experiences. A relationship built on inconsistency or negativity won't last long.

Your *presence* is how you show up and present yourself to the world—it's how *you do you*. Presence can be tied to external things, such as how you dress. But it's also defined by how you choose to be viewed in various settings. It's defined by the energy and emotions you bring to a situation, whether at work, at home, with friends, or in your community. Your presence also involves how and what you share on social media. Like it or not, impressions are created, and brands are defined based on how people present themselves. The important thing to remember about presence, personal or professional, is that it shouldn't mask the truth. It's hard work to consistently pretend to be someone else. At some point, people will see through the lie.

When it comes to the *description* of your personal brand, keep in mind that this description isn't yours. It's how others describe you and what it's like to be in a personal or professional relationship with you. The way others describe you indicates whether you're viewed as authentic and true to yourself. Powerful personal brands influence others. They have it going on. If a description of you seems off the mark, this is a wake-up call—an opportunity to figure out why there's a disconnect between how you view yourself and how others view you.

## Sample Brand Authenticity Examples

As an example, I'll share with you my assessment of the brand authenticity of two people. First, I selected a significant person in my personal life—my father. Second, I selected a person in my professional life—Sam (introduced in Chapter 1, *Authentic Leadership).* Bear in mind that, as in the Apple example, the ratings are based on my point of view.

As I've covered, authentic personal brands clearly convey what matters to them. In order to understand what matters to another person, you need to be in a personal or professional relationship with them. You have a picture in your head of what it's like to be in a relationship with the people in your life and who you believe they are at the core. The scoring system is meant to capture what you know about them through the six brand attributes. Obviously, it's possible that you are unclear about some of the brand attributes or what matters to the other person. That's the point. Authentic brands are clear and consistent.

Here's the scoring system again.

**Scoring system:**

2 This attribute is clear and delivered consistently

1 This attribute is somewhat clear and sometimes delivered

0 This attribute is unclear and not delivered

**MY FATHER:**

| **Attributes** | **My point of view** |
|---|---|
| **Purpose**<br>*the why in his life* | My father takes care of his family through hard work, love, support, encouragement, and being there when needed. He supports friends and neighbors in times of need.<br><br>**My rating: 2.** My father's purpose is clear to me. |
| **Promise**<br>*what commitments exist* | My father never wavered in his commitment to my mother, caring for her right up to her death and setting an example of love and devotion.<br><br>**My rating: 2.** My father delivers on his promises. |
| **Principles**<br>*demonstrated values* | Devotion, commitment, strong work ethic, and unconditional love.<br><br>**My rating: 2.** My father lives these values. |
| **Experiences**<br>*interactions throughout the relationship* | My father makes us laugh, gives the best bear hugs, shares his wisdom, and works hard without complaint. He's a role model for his kids and grandkids.<br><br>**My rating: 2.** My experiences with him have been consistant |
| **Presence**<br>*how he shows up* | He is humble and approachable. He wears a suit or camouflage equally well. He has endless energy for family and chores–until he collapses in front of the TV!<br><br>**My rating: 2.** My father shows up and presents himself with energy and enthusiasm. Did I mention that he irons his jeans? |
| **Description**<br>*how I talk about the brand* | My father is loving, has a great sense of humor, and is the most important example of a leader in my life.<br><br>**My rating: 2.** I've always wanted to be like my father. He's loved and respected and has a clear, consistent brand. |

**My Father – Score: 12/12**

I believe my father deserves the highest possible score for living his brand with authenticity and purpose. He leads his family in a manner that's consistent with what matters most to him. My father lives his life focused on his True North. All who meet him are clear on his True North as well.

Now I'll share my point of view about Sam, with whom I had a professional relationship. Recall that Sam behaved as if he were the smartest person in the room and was promoted to a role outside his skillset and level of experience.

**SAM:**

| **Attributes** | **My point of view** |
|---|---|
| **Purpose**<br>*the why of its existence* | Why did Sam behave the way he did? Was he was trying to impose his authority on his new team? Trying to impress his leader? Modeling what he thought it would take to become successful in his role?<br><br>**My rating: 0.** His purpose was unclear. |
| **Promise**<br>*what customers should expect* | Sam was committed to his approach and his approach alone. No one else's ideas and opinions mattered. Unfortunately, we didn't trust him to deliver on any promises.<br><br>**My rating: 0.** His promise was unclear. |
| **Principles**<br>*what the business values* | Ambition, power, authority, and control<br><br>**My rating: 2.** Sam demonstrated these principles consistently. |
| **Experiences**<br>*the interactions people have with the brand* | My relationship with Sam was defined by negative experiences, so I chose to eliminate him from my life.<br><br>**My rating: 0.** I don't view Sam as someone who desired to create positive meaningful relationships in business. |
| **Presence**<br>*how it's presented to the world* | Sam dressed the part but his appearance was only one factor. Sam's controlling ways were de-energizing, and the most common emotion he created was stress.<br><br>**My rating: 0.** Sam's presence was detrimental to others. |
| **Description**<br>*how I talk about the brand* | Sam appeared to be a power hungry leader whose actions caused employees to disengage.<br><br>**My rating: 2**. Why the score of 2? This attribute was clear and delivered consistently. |

**SAM – Score: 4/12**

Sam scored low on the authenticity scale because his personal brand doesn't clearly convey what matters to him. He doesn't lead with authenticity and purpose. Sam might be a wonderful person at heart, but he doesn't bring that person to work. Those around him don't feel that they matter to Sam, and their experiences with him are the basis for their perceptions.

My rating of Sam might appear tough, but my intent isn't to bash him. I believe in the general goodness of people. My perception of Sam is that he's struggling with misconceptions about leadership based on experiences he had in his youth. Something powerful is causing Sam to believe he needs to behave the way he does to earn the respect of his team and his leader. Until Sam gets in touch with what matters to him and comes to terms with his personal brand, he won't change. Turnover in his department, a demotion, or getting fired could be catalysts that prompt his desire to understand what's happening.

Normally you wouldn't use a chart to rate another person—and I wouldn't encourage that. But this is a way for you to compare and contrast what is clear and unclear about personal brands you know before you turn the lens inward on your own personal brand, which you'll do in a later chapter. These examples should help make the point clearer.

Whether business or personal, a brand lives in the eyes of those who are in a relationship with the brand.

## Brand Preference and Resonance

We make choices about business brands every day. Often, we'll try a brand because someone we trust recommended it or it has several five-star ratings and positive reviews. In some cases, we care deeply about a brand's mission, so we commit to that brand, regardless of price—it just feels like the right thing to do.

We all prefer different things. This is why both Starbucks and Dunkin' Donuts exist. I'd like to think that if these companies were people, they could have a nice conversation about the similarities and differences in their purposes and promises. And they could both be happy that the caffeine needs of so many are being met.

We've all written off certain business brands because of poor quality, because we had a negative experience, or because we found something we think is better. Regardless, in most cases it's not personal—it's preference. The brand no longer resonates with our needs, tastes, or desires.

For instance, I love shopping at Wegmans. The experiences I have in this family-owned supermarket far exceed those I've had at any other supermarket. The products, staff, and general appearance of the store are consistently positive. I'll drive past several competitors to shop at Wegmans. This is my preference.

Even if a brand meets all the criteria of authenticity, it won't resonate with everyone. Strong brands are clear on who their target audience is. They recognize that they're not all things to all people.

The same is true in terms of personal brands. When individuals are true to themselves, they're bound to resonate with some people and not others. We choose to spend time with certain people based on the experiences we have with them, the way they make us feel, and how connected we feel to what they stand for. That said, we can still connect with people with whom we don't agree. We can respect them and appreciate their uniqueness.

## Find what Resonates

My business partner, Dave, has had a successful career as an executive, entrepreneur, and author. Shortly into our time working together at Raymour & Flanigan Furniture, he told me about the time when he was fired early in his career. Dave had been president of a family-owned paper company. Although he was proud of his many accomplishments in the role, he realized that his leadership style no longer resonated with the owners.

When Dave tells the story, he says, "Getting fired was the best thing that could have happened!" The thing about Dave is that he's comfortable in his own skin. He knows exactly who he is and what matters most to him. He didn't take it personally. In fact, he recognized that he was no longer a fit long before the day he was fired. He and the CEO parted ways on good terms and remained friends.

Dave went on to a role that was much more in line with who he is as a leader—with what matters to him personally and professionally. He considers the termination a great lesson. I have to admit, when he shared this story, I was awestruck by how he handled getting fired. I admired him and felt a strong desire to become clearer about what mattered to me, so I could weather a storm like that if I ever needed to.

None of us wants to feel vulnerable or rejected, but confidence and authenticity are strong armor. This lesson reinforced my personal mission to be clear about my brand and help others do the same.

## Some People Won't Like You

Get over it. If you picked up this book in the hopes of creating a brand that everyone loves, you'll be disappointed. Successful branding isn't about creating a persona or being a chameleon. To be true to yourself and your brand, you need to be consistent. Don't change yourself to fit a relationship or situation. Be comfortable and confident in your own skin.

One day I was shopping and saw an outfit on a mannequin that I felt would make me look younger, hip, and trendy. "I can pull that off!" I thought, despite the fact it was clearly not my style. As soon as I put it on, I felt silly. It wasn't me. If I'd been with my daughter, Jessica, who has a sharp wit and is always direct, she'd give me a look and say, "Uh, seriously? No!"

Being comfortable in your own skin is different from picking out the wrong outfit, but it's a metaphor that many of us can relate to. When our external persona doesn't fit, our inner discomfort is very real. Acting takes effort and is ultimately draining. If you're in a situation that's causing you to compromise your values, or you're modeling behaviors to fit in, your stress levels will be high.

All through high school and part of college, I worked at McDonald's. I held just about every position: drive-through attendant, cashier, biscuit-maker, etc. I worked the grill, opened, closed, and cleaned. I spent years in a greasy green polyester uniform and a visor that gave my big eighties hair terrible hat-head. But aside from hating that uniform, I was proud of my job. It allowed me to purchase my first car, pay for my own school clothes, and partially pay for college. I had no intention of staying in the fast-food business as a career, but I worked hard, did my best, and put a smile on my face—even on those days when a fellow employee shouted those dreaded words, "A bus just arrived!"

After completing two years of college, I was shopping in a Dick's Sporting Goods store and ran into one of my previous managers from McDonald's. He was now managing at Dick's and, recalling that I was creative, told me about a job vacancy. The role would involve making signs for all the locations and reporting to the director of stores. I needed to fund my way through college, and this sounded interesting. I liked the idea of leveraging my creative skills and working in something other than a polyester uniform.

My former manager recommended me to the director and told him what a hard worker I was. I applied, interviewed with the director of stores, Bill Colombo, and got the job. Bill, whom you met in Chapter 1, *Authentic Leadership*, proved to be a mentor who helped shape me as a leader. I'm grateful every day that I had that opportunity. It launched my marketing career.

I've shared this story with my kids many times. Relationships matter. Had I not given it my all at McDonald's, I wouldn't have been recommended for the career-shaping job at Dick's Sporting Goods. I wouldn't have met my mentor, Bill, and I wouldn't have learned all the valuable lessons he taught me. What we do and how we do it, the experiences we create with others, and the way they describe us—all these things have a significant impact on our brands.

## Brand Authenticity Exercise

Take a few moments to rate brands in your personal and professional life. Select brands that are important to you. The business brand could be a product, service, retailer, or organization that you feel strongly about. The personal brand could be someone you wrote about in the exercises in Chapter 2, *Determine What Matters*. Rate the brand's authenticity using the same scoring system I used in the examples presented earlier in this chapter.

Grab the companion workbook you downloaded from www.danelipartners.com/books/justdoyou to capture your answers.

**Scoring system:**

2 This attribute is clear and delivered consistently

1 This attribute is somewhat clear and sometimes delivered

0 This attribute is unclear and not delivered

**PERSONAL BRAND:**

| Attributes | My point of view |
|---|---|
| **Purpose**<br>*the why in their life* | My rating: ____ |
| **Promise**<br>*what commitments exist* | My rating: ____ |
| **Principles**<br>*demonstrated values* | My rating: ____ |
| **Experiences**<br>*interactions throughout the relationship* | My rating: ____ |
| **Presence**<br>*how they show up* | My rating: ____ |
| **Description**<br>*how I talk about the brand* | My rating: ____ |

**Personal Brand Score: /12**

**BUSINESS BRAND:**

| Attributes | My point of view |
|---|---|
| **Purpose**<br>*the why of its existence* | My rating: ____ |
| **Promise**<br>*what customers should expect* | My rating: ____ |
| **Principles**<br>*what the business values* | My rating: ____ |
| **Experiences**<br>*interactions people have with the brand* | My rating: ____ |
| **Presence**<br>*how it's presented to the world* | My rating: ____ |
| **Description**<br>*how I talk about the brand* | My rating: ____ |

**Business Brand Score: /12**

Remember: accept when your brand doesn't resonate. It's not personal—it's just a preference. Choose you.

Throughout your journey as a leader, I hope you stay focused on *what* and *who* matters most to you. Life is full of stress, challenges, and unexpected situations. But what you can control is yourself, how you react to things, and the experiences you create with those who matter to you. Authenticity is what people notice, what they respond to, and what builds influence.

## Authentic Branding: Summary

Business brands and personal brands are measured in similar ways. Both are defined by relationships. Authentic relationships are built when a brand:

- Has a clear *purpose*
- Keeps its *promise*
- Adheres to its *principles*
- Provides *experiences* that are consistently fulfilling

- Has a *presence* that's genuine
- Matches the *description* others give it

When you completed the brand authenticity exercise, you likely chose particular business and personal brands because they're important in your life—because they're authentic and they've influenced you. They move into a leadership position in your mind because they outperform other brands. You place a high value on them and are loyal to them. Even if there are issues with these brands or they make mistakes, you have confidence in your relationship with them and believe these things can be overcome. The authenticity of these brands is clear to those who interact with them. They are focused on their True North.

Remember, we all have preferences, and some brands will resonate with us while others won't. When brands are authentic and their attributes are consistently demonstrated, they are powerful and influential—even if they aren't loved by all. It's impossible to be all things to all people, so being authentic is the key to fulfillment.

In the next chapter, you'll define your personal brand by connecting what matters to you to your brand attributes.

## Chapter 4

# Connect to Who You Are

*Only the truth of who you are, if realized, will set you free.*

Eckhardt Tolle

It's time to take a close look at your principles (what you value), your promises (what others can expect from you), and your purpose (your why).

In this chapter, you will learn:

- How to activate what matters
- What commitments will define your leadership brand
- How to define your purpose

When you worked through the questions using the metacognitive process in Chapter 2, *Determine What Matters*, you likely uncovered critical life lessons and experiences you haven't thought about in a long time—or maybe ever. Reflecting on life experiences helps to reveal what matters deeply to you, what you want to avoid, and the kind of person you want to be. Behaviors are shaped by both good and bad lessons. You can choose to move forward from these lessons in a way that represents your authentic self.

You've also been introduced to the concept of authentic personal branding and why aligning with your True North will help you make decisions. With this knowledge, you can clearly define the attributes of your personal brand.

It's deep within your life experiences and resulting behaviors that your core principles are revealed, the inspiration for your promises exists, and your purpose is defined. Consider how these three brand attributes impact all aspects of your personal and professional life. In order to lead with authenticity, you need to be very clear on these three things.

Capture your responses in your *Just Do You* companion workbook: visit www.danelipartners.com/books/justdoyou to download now.

Be sure to have your responses from Chapter 2, *Determine What Matters*, available to reference as you work through this chapter.

## Principles

Your principles are the embodiment of what you value. You develop them over time and through your life experiences. Some are based on positive experiences and deep beliefs. Others are defined as a result of something negative or traumatic.

Many people don't clearly articulate their principles. They're drawn to things but don't consciously determine why these things fulfill them. But when you define your principles clearly, you create passion and enthusiasm around what you're doing—or seek to do. And in doing so, you take action with clarity. Decisions become easier because they can be measured against alignment with principles.

We're going to use a Venn diagram to capture your core principles in three areas: personal, professional, and aspirational. You'll define principles for all these aspects of your life in order to see the commonalities and differences.

Here's an example of a completed Venn diagram. It's populated with personal, professional, and aspirational core principles.

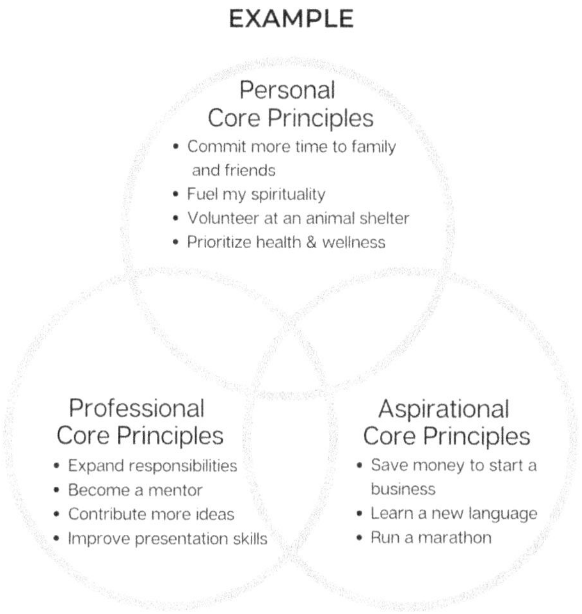

**EXAMPLE**



## Personal Core Principles

Your truths, beliefs, and passions are revealed in your responses to the questions in Chapter 2, *Determine What Matters*. The personal experiences you revisited hold the key to what matters to you in your personal relationships.

- *Early life and influences.* Think about the leaders who influenced you deeply in your youth and consider why they were important to your development. Recall what you carried forward and how your behaviors evolved as a result
- *Self-awareness.* Refer to the people you identified as most important to you in your personal life. Next, consider the

commitments you identified as really important to you and the things that bother you

- *Career and aspirations.* In thinking about what you want to achieve long term, you connect to what motivates you. Achieving your aspirational goals means connecting your passion and energy to what you want to do in life

## Professional Core Principles

The goals and achievements that are important to you in your life's work can be drawn from your experiences and the lessons you learned from the leaders in your past.

- *Early life and influences.* Think about the leaders who embody the traits you most admire. Equally important, the traits of the leaders you consider to be less effective or damaging. Refer to your defining moments and what you learned about yourself
- *Self-awareness.* Refer to the people you identified as most important to you in your professional life. Also revisit your responses to the questions about what you do and why you do it. Consider how you can better link your efforts with work that makes you burst with energy
- *Career and aspirations.* You identified your goals for this year as well as for two, five, and ten years into the future. You also determined your barriers and the best areas in which to invest your time and energy to ensure future success. Refer to those responses for insights

## Aspirational Core Principles

Be bold, be courageous, and define a future state that you dream of achieving. Consider how you'll make your mark on the world and embody what matters in all you do.

- *Early life and influences.* Think about who has inspired you to dream more, learn more, do more, and become more. What has their example taught you and what do you intend to do about it?

- *Self-awareness.* As you reflect on your responses to what affects you deeply, consider how you convey this in your social media presence. Are you sharing or liking things that relate to your aspirations?
- *Career and aspirations.* When you allowed yourself to dream about what you would do for a living if money weren't a factor, you likely discovered your deepest aspiration. Revisit this dream

In your workbook you'll find a blank Venn diagram for you to populate with your own core principles. What are your personal, professional, and aspirational core principles? How would you complete the Venn diagram?

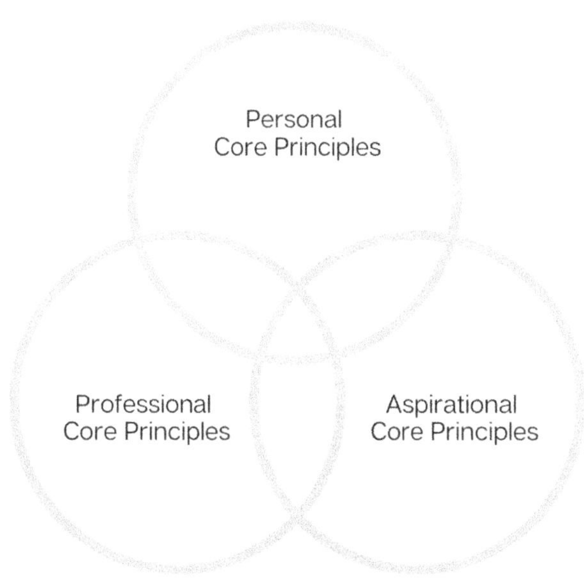


Once you've populated the Venn diagram with what matters most to you from a personal, professional, and aspirational perspective, take a moment to reflect. Do the things you listed stand up against the definition of principles? Again, your principles embody what you value. They're developed over time and through your life experiences. These strong inner feelings about right and wrong have the power to call you to action.

Make sure what you've listed feels right. If anything feels a bit off, return to your responses in Chapter 2, *Determine What Matters*, and make changes where necessary.

## The Nexus

The point at which your personal, professional, and aspirational core principles intersect is the nexus. This is the essence of who you are. Again, in your workbook you'll find space to craft your own nexus statement.

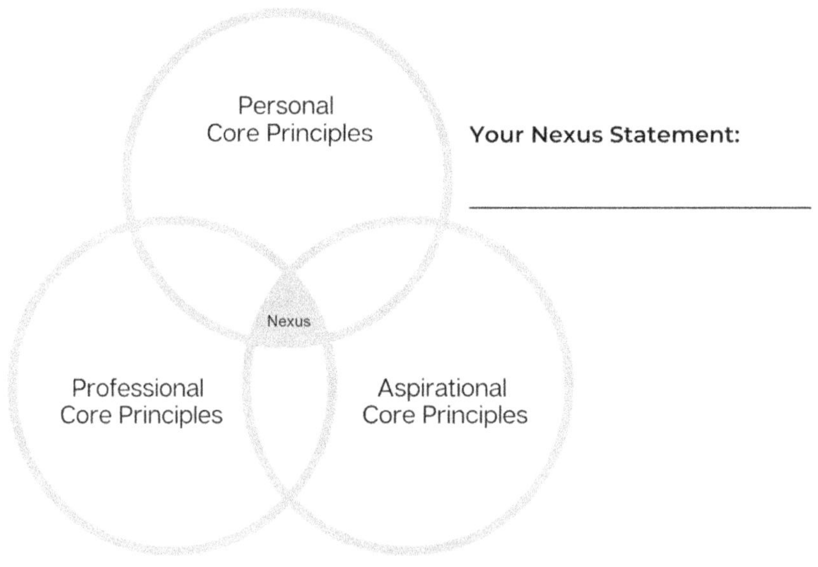

Here are some examples of nexus statements:

- I'm a caregiver
- I'm an artist; I want to bring beauty to others
- I care deeply about the environment
- I'm a learning enthusiast; new people and experiences energize me
- I'm a teacher and mentor; I empower others

## Promise

Promises are a way of telling people what to expect. You commit to doing something for someone else. Affection and trust are built on promises kept. Broken promises destroy trust. And a lack of trust can end relationships.

If an employee fails to deliver on promises, it's only a matter of time until they're demoted or out of a job. If trust has been developed because promises are consistently kept, mistakes or slips can be forgiven. When trust is lost, relationships are permanently damaged.

The next step in your personal discovery is to establish what you intend to do for yourself and others. Define your promises and consider what they mean to your personal and professional relationships. This is your nonnegotiable list of commitments. They will shape your decisions and actions from this point forward.

Here are some examples of promises:

- To myself: I promise to make time to exercise at least three times weekly because my health matters to me.
- To my personal relationships: I'll do my best to go offline on weekends so I am present for my family
- To the people who matter to me in my professional relationships: whenever possible, I'll contribute to projects outside my normal responsibilities in an effort to collaborate with others, to learn, and to grow

- To my future self: I'll learn all I can in my current role and will seek ways to overcome barriers so I can achieve my goal of starting my own business

Now it's your turn.

My promise to myself:

My promise to the people who matter to me in my personal relationships:

My promise to the people who matter to me in my professional relationships:

My promise to my future self (in regard to aspirations):

Writing your commitments to yourself and others makes them real. Once you've defined promises that you feel confident you can deliver on, I recommend sharing them with the people for whom they're intended. If you're concerned about your ability to deliver on the commitments as stated, add phrases such as the ones used in the examples (e.g., *whenever possible* and *will do my best*). Remember, trust is established in relationships through consistent delivery of promises, so be sure your words and intentions match your actions.

## Purpose

You're nearly finished! The final step in this chapter is to create your purpose statement.

Your purpose defines you. It's a bold statement that summarizes your gifts and what you desire to achieve—your reason for being.

Your purpose statement must align with what matters to you, be consistent with your core principles, and allow you to deliver on your promises. Allow time for reflection and compose a draft or two. Begin to determine what truly resonates with you. Choose positive action words so your statement has power and energy. It doesn't need to be longer than a sentence or two.

As you construct the statement, it might be helpful to consider the following questions:

- What makes me unique?
- What do I do? What will I do?
- Whom do I aim to serve? What are their needs?
- What is my desired outcome? What legacy do I want to leave?

Here are some examples of purpose statements:

- My purpose statement: "*To use my strengths and experience to pay it forward by giving the gift that was given to me by all the great leaders in my life.*"

- Oprah Winfrey's purpose statement: "*To be a teacher. And to be known for inspiring my students to be more than they thought they could be.*[1]"

- Sir Richard Branson's purpose statement: "*To have fun in [my] journey through life and learn from [my] mistakes.*"[2]

- Amanda Steinberg's purpose statement: "*To use my gifts of intelligence, charisma, and serial optimism to cultivate the self-worth and net-worth of women around the world.*"[3]

What is my purpose statement?

## Connect to Who You Are: Summary

Congratulations! You've identified your personal, professional, and aspirational core principles, determined the promises you're committed to making to yourself and others, and crafted your purpose statement. Your personal brand is taking shape.

When you visualize these attributes (principles, promises, purpose), you breathe life into them. The Venn diagram is a tool you can keep referring to as a reminder of what you value and what you're working toward. Your promises to yourself and the important people in your life will keep you focused and inspire others. And your purpose statement will define your why from this point forward. All six brand attributes, when authentically demonstrated, keep you facing in the direction of what matters. They're a compass pointing to your True North.

In the next chapter, we'll explore the other three brand attributes: experiences, presence, and description.

## Chapter 5

# See Who Others See

> *Your brand is what others say about you when you're not in the room.*
>
> Jeff Bezos

Let's dig into the more external attributes of your personal brand: experiences, presence, and description. These are the attributes that express what matters to you and show others how "you do you." Perhaps you think about these attributes often. Or maybe you've never explored how they represent who you are and how they impact others.

You've defined your purpose, promises, and principles, so thinking about how these attributes are conveyed to others is a key step in the development of your personal brand.

In this chapter, you will:

- Examine the experiences you're creating with others
- Consider what your presence looks like
- Determine whether the current description of you is in alignment with your brand

I've posed questions throughout this chapter. Grab your companion workbook and write your answers there. Don't have your workbook yet? Head over to www.danelipartners.com/books/justdoyou to grab it now.

## Experiences

The interactions you have in your personal and professional relationships define how people feel about you. They also tell others how you feel about them. We naturally gravitate toward people who provide consistent and positive experiences.

Experiences are made up of small interactions, the ones I call micro moments. The micro moments are the day-to-day interactions with others that occur without much thought—like when you leave home in the morning, or return home after work, when you pass a colleague in the hallway, when you run into someone at the coffee shop, or say hello (or not) to a neighbor when you grab your mail. They add up to create a picture of you. Consider how you behave in your micro-moments, when you're on autopilot.

The profound moments happen less often but can have a more lasting impact. These times in your life stand out as pivotal if you show up for them as your whole self, or, conversely, if you don't show up and end up missing an opportunity to create a desired experience.

## Offer Your Whole Self

As I reflect on profound personal experiences in my life, I'm taken back to the last few days of my mother's life. In the spring and summer of 2018, her health was deteriorating and she was in and out of the hospital. After what would be my mother's final trip home from the hospital, I stayed with may parents for a few days to help out.

Mom needed twenty-four-hour care and I wanted to help around the house, make meals, and give my father breaks. The day after I returned to my home, my mother passed away in her sleep. She and my father stayed up most of that night talking, and when he turned away to get something for her, she lay her head on her pillow and drifted off.

Throughout everything she endured, her attitude was one of strength and positivity. She remained optimistic for her family and never let on how poorly she was feeling. Even in her final days, she refused to admit she was going to die. She'd say, "I'm not going anywhere—I have too much to live for!" I sat in her room with her for three days talking about my kids, sharing the things going on in my life, and watching her favorite daytime television shows. I yearned to say some things that I felt needed to be said. I wanted her to know how much I loved her and admired her strength. I wanted to resolve some things from our past. I wanted her to know things about me that I'd never told her. I wanted her to know that she'd be missed. I didn't say any of that, and I'll regret it until the day I die. I didn't feel that I could have an end-of-life conversation with her because she was so determined that she wasn't going anywhere. But I missed an opportunity that I'll never get back. I was there, helping and talking, but I didn't offer my whole self.

## Colleagues and Comrades

I witnessed a friendship grow into something powerful between two colleagues on my team. Jeff and Barry had worked together for a few years. Jeff is structured and analytical and Barry is creative and free-spirited. After trust was built in their relationship, Jeff confided that he and his wife had been trying for years to adopt a child. They were feeling discouraged and losing hope. Barry, a brilliant designer, helped Jeff and his wife redesign their adoption profile. He made it personal, expressing who they were and what mattered to them. When the rest of the team learned about their friendship and how they were working together, everyone was moved. It brought us all together.

Barry and Jeff set an example of connecting what matters to the workplace in a way that made a difference in their lives as well as in the lives of everyone else on the team. And yes, Jeff and Nancy adopted a beautiful baby boy.

In professional settings, it may seem difficult to bring your whole self and share what matters. But doing so can yield incredible results.

## Experiences Reflection

Think about the interactions you have in your **personal** relationships. Consider a specific profound moment. Ask yourself:

Was this moment all I wanted it to be?

What were the circumstances that made it great or difficult?

What was important or memorable about it?

How do I feel about it now?

How would I change that moment if I could?

Next, consider your *micro moments*. Ask yourself:

How am I perceived when I'm on autopilot?

Do the people I've identified as important to me in my personal life know they are important through my regular actions?

Think about the interactions you have in your **professional** relationships. Consider a specific profound moment. Ask yourself:

Was this moment all I wanted it to be?

What were the circumstances that made it great or difficult?

What was important or memorable about it?

How do I feel about it now?

How would I change that moment if I could?

Next, consider your *micro moments*. Ask yourself:

How am I perceived when I'm on autopilot?

Do the people I've identified as important to me in my professional I life know they are important through my regular actions?

## Presence

Presence is all about how you show up. What you wear, what you do on social media, and the energy and emotion you bring to a situation all play a role in defining your presence. Like it or not, these factors contribute to the impression of your overall brand. People will form opinions about you based on your appearance—it's not about having designer clothing but about dressing appropriately for the situation. Your social media profile will tell others a lot about who you are and what you care about. But your energy and emotion will have the greatest impact on how your presence is perceived.

## Business Presence

Many issues can arise based on perception. For instance, in a business setting, I pride myself on being early and prepared for meetings. So when I attend meetings where people show up late, slouch, and multitask when someone is speaking, I chalk them up as disrespectful and disengaged. My perception of these people is formed based on what I witness. Their energy is low and they don't seem to care about being here or about how they present themselves. Is my assessment fair? I'm not sure. How they show up and my resulting perception translate into doubts about their overall job performance. If they have low energy and are disrespectful and disengaged in a room full of people, how can I expect them to work hard when alone?

On the flip side, when someone enters a room with high energy and is engaged, the whole vibe of the meeting changes. Their contribution adds value. I perceive this person as wanting to be here and collaborate, and as someone who respects others' time. This matters in a professional setting.

It also matters that your appearance meets your company's expectations. There's much more flexibility today regarding business attire than there was when I started my career. Suits were the norm back then, and this actually made things easier because there was no question about what was right or wrong. Now, many environments are casual, particularly if it's a creative environment—jeans and T-shirts are often acceptable. Some companies have a *use your best judgment* guideline. Even with all this change, I believe the old rule of *dress for the role you want, not the one you have* is the right approach. Look at the leadership in your organization to understand what's acceptable. If you want to be perceived as being serious about your role and getting to a leadership position, looking the part is important. Demonstrate that you want to be invited to more client meetings and that you're prepared and dressed to do just that.

## Personal Presence

In your personal life, your presence is less about what you wear and more about the energy and emotion you bring to your relationships. How you show up for those who mean the most to you really matters. There have been times in my life where I've left all my energy in the office and gone home physically and emotionally drained. It happens to all of us. If it's an occasional occurrence, it won't leave a lasting impression. However, if you frequently feel low energy levels in your personal relationships, you'll want to consider the cause. We'll cover more of this in Chapter 7, *Identify Conflicts*.

The emotion you bring to a situation is also a result of how true you're being to yourself and whether you feel as if you're fulfilling your purpose. Presence in the form of positive energy is inspiring and energizes others. Conversely, negative energy from you when you're feeling misaligned can unintentionally bring others down. If those closest to you empathize with you, they may feel what you're feeling and try to meet you where you are.

## Your Online Presence

Our ability to create online personas and connect with people around the world is remarkable. The opportunities and risks are real. What we share helps define who we are and how the world perceives us.

We've all seen it—those people on social media who create online personas that don't feel consistent with who you know them to be. The images they share, the words they post, and the experiences they identify as most meaningful fall short of who you see when you interact with them in person. This is disingenuous at best. They're certainly not portraying their authentic selves. This kind of inconsistency may be driven by a desire to compete with others, or to be seen as living a purposeful life. It could be the result of insecurity or a need to be "liked." Or, maybe it comes from a need to fit in a particular social circle. Regardless, a person's social media profile creates perceptions about who they are and who they aren't.

. . .

What does this mean for your brand? Well, you and your social media profiles *are* your brand. If that scares you, then you have some work to do. When we share something on social media, we open a window into our world and invite everyone to look in.

## Presence Reflection

Think about how you show up in a professional setting:

Am I fully present and prepared?

Am I aloof and distracted?

Do I dress appropriately for the situation?

Do I behave in a way that shows my colleagues and leader I'm engaged?

Think about how you show up in a personal setting:

Am I fully present emotionally for those who matter most to me?

Do I bring the energy I want to my relationships?

What's the mood when I enter a room?

Do I behave in a way that shows my family and friends I'm engaged?

Think about your social media profiles:

Do my social media profiles present a clear picture of me?

Does my social media presence match my professional presence?

Does my social media presence match my personal presence?

Is there anyone in my personal or professional life whom I would NOT want to see some of my social media activity?

## Description

As we discussed in Chapter 3, *Authentic Branding,* from a branding perspective the description of you is not your own. The way others articulate who you are is all about the relationship they have with you and what they believe they know about you. If their description of you is off the mark, it can serve as a wake-up call.

One way to get a sense of your current description is to review a reference or comments in a performance review. Or, if you've ever requested a recommendation through LinkedIn, you'll have specific examples of a description of you from someone else's point of view. I learned a lot about myself when I requested recommendations every time I changed jobs. It was like looking in the rearview mirror and getting a clear sense of my brand.

Another way to consider your description from another's point of view is to think about a time when someone introduced you in a professional setting. Did the person just use your name and title? Or did they elaborate and share more about you or your work? A basic introduction might sound something like this: "This is Beth. She's a web designer." But if the person had seen more of Beth's brand, they might say: "This is Beth. She's passionate about her work and ensures our customers have the best possible experience on our website."

Now that you've done the hard work to define your purpose, promises, and principles, consider how you might want to reframe the way others describe you. What's your ideal description of yourself? To determine this, picture yourself in a situation where you're meeting someone new. You're standing next to someone who's important to you, and it's up to this person to make the introduction. What do you want them to say about you? How do you hope to be described in a brief statement?

In your companion workbook, write a description of yourself that reflects your unique attributes and invites others to get to know your authentic self. Give people a glimpse into what matters to you.

What is my preferred description? How do I want to be introduced?

## See Who Others See: Summary

Your brand's external attributes are what others see and respond to. The experiences you create, your presence, and your description should all reflect what's inside you. If they don't, then you need to consider how you'll correct your course.

The experiences you create through micro-moments and profound moments have the power to build trust and lasting, meaningful relationships. How you show up in a situation (the energy and emotion you bring) defines your presence and creates a perception of who you are and how much you care. If you're living authentically, others will describe you accurately.

With greater self-awareness and a better understanding of your personal brand, you can now focus on becoming more of who you are for those who matter most.

In the next chapter, armed with the knowledge you've gained from all the exercises you've completed so far you'll complete one final exercise: you'll rate your personal brand.

# Chapter 6
# Examine Your Personal Brand

> *Authenticity is a collection of choices that we have to make every day. It's about the choice to show up and be real.*
>
> Brené Brown

You've completed all the exercises related to the six brand attributes. Now it's time to rate your brand. The exercise in this chapter will tie together everything you've learned so far and challenge you to assess where you are in relation to where you want to be, based on your new self-awareness.

Be sure to take your time working through this so you have a clear picture of where your brand is today. This isn't a pass or fail exercise. It's an honest assessment of where you are so you can determine where you want to go.

Examining your personal brand can be a difficult process, as it requires objectivity. As you work through the exercise in this chapter, you may want to ask trusted people in your life to provide additional insights.

. . .

In this chapter, you will:

- Consider how authentic your brand is today
- Rate your six brand attributes
- Understand your gap areas
- Determine your leadership-developmental needs

## How Authentic is Your Personal Brand?

Determining the authenticity of your personal brand is critical if you want to live and lead with authenticity and purpose. You need clarity on how your brand intersects with what matters to you.

In the following exercise, we'll examine all the aspects of your brand's authenticity through the lens of your personal and professional relationships. Use your companion workbook to record your answers, or get it here: www.danelipartners.com/books/justdoyou.

First, refer to the *who matters most to me* lists you created in Chapter 2, *Determine What Matters*. Consider the following exercises from their point of view.

Who matters most to me in my personal life?

Who matters most to me in my academic or professional life?

We'll use the same scoring system introduced in Chapter 3, *Authentic Branding*.

**Scoring system:**
2 – [Yes] I'm clear and deliver consistently
1 – [Maybe] I'm somewhat clear and sometimes deliver
0 – [No] I'm unclear and I'm not delivering

| **PURPOSE**<br>The essence of what I do for others | |
|---|---|
| My family members are aware of my gifts and what I'm passionate about | **My Score:** |
| My closest friends are aware of my gifts and what I'm passionate about | **My Score:** |
| My colleagues and leaders are aware of my gifts and what I'm passionate about | **My Score:** |
| My work closely aligns with my purpose | **My Score:** |
| I'm learning and doing things that move me toward fulfilling my purpose | **My Score:** |
| | **TOTAL:** |

| **PROMISE**<br>How I meet commitments and expectations | |
|---|---|
| I deliver on my promises to my family | **My Score:** |
| I deliver on my promises to my friends | **My Score:** |
| I deliver on my promises at work | **My Score:** |
| I deliver on my promises to myself | **My Score:** |
| | **TOTAL:** |

| **PRINCIPLES**<br>The embodiment of what I value deeply | |
|---|---|
| I'm clear about what I value | **My Score:** |
| My family is clear about what I value | **My Score:** |
| My friends are clear about what I value | **My Score:** |
| My colleagues/leaders are clear about my values | **My Score:** |
| | **TOTAL:** |

| **EXPERIENCES**<br>The interactions I create | |
|---|---|
| My interactions with my family demonstrate my purpose and principles | **My Score:** |
| My interactions with my friends demonstrate my purpose and principles | **My Score:** |
| My interactions at work demonstrate my purpose and principles | **My Score:** |
| My interactions with people I've just met demonstrate my purpose and principles | **My Score:** |
| | **TOTAL:** |

| **PRESENCE**<br>The genuine representation of who I am | |
|---|---|
| I share the real me with family | **My Score:** |
| I share the real me with friends | **My Score:** |
| I share the real me at work | **My Score:** |
| I share the real me on social media | **My Score:** |
| | **TOTAL:** |

| **DESCRIPTION**<br>The accurate description of who I am | |
|---|---|
| My family would describe me using the same words or phrases I would | **My Score:** |
| My friends would describe me using the same words or phrases I would | **My Score:** |
| My colleagues and leaders would describe me using the same words or phrases I would | **My Score:** |
| If someone met me briefly, they would get an accurate snapshot of who I am | **My Score:** |
| | **TOTAL:** |

Now, add up all the totals to determine the authenticity of your brand.

**YOUR SCORE:**

| Grand Total | What this means |
|---|---|
| **0–15** | You've identified many areas that require your focus if you wish to lead with authenticity and purpose |
| **16–29** | Some areas of your life are aligned with your True North, but you've identified some gap areas that require your focus |
| **30-44** | You have clarity and have identified the areas you need to refine. You're well on your way! |
| **45-50** | Congratulations! You're living your brand and have perhaps identified a few areas to tweak |

The first step in any process where change is required is to identify issues and opportunities. Now that you've done that, the remaining chapters in this book will guide you through steps to help you correct your course. I've also included a list of recommended reading at the end of the book if you need additional help aligning with your True North and addressing potential gap areas or leadership development needs.

Take a few moments to note these gaps or needs before you move on to the next chapter. This will come in handy later as you consider how you want to move forward.

## Examine Your Personal Brand: Summary

Brands are defined by relationships. The authenticity of your brand is determined by those in personal and professional relationships with you. If you're bringing the real you to your relationships, you'll be seen as authentic. The six brand attributes allow you to measure your brand's authenticity as well as your commitment to what matters most to you.

The exercises have likely been eye-opening. Don't get discouraged if you identified gap areas or developmental needs. We all have things we need to focus on, and greater self-awareness will help you redirect your course.

In Part Three, *Your True North*, you'll identify conflicts and discover ways to return to your True North when life unexpectedly throws you off track.

## Key Takeaways, Part Two

### BRANDS AND WHY THEY MATTER

- The Venn diagram you populated is a tool you can refer back to as a reminder of what you value and what you're working toward. It can be updated as your priorities change—for instance, as your family grows, as you change jobs, or as your interests evolve

- Your promises to yourself and the other important people in your life should be shared and updated as circumstances change. Your commitments will keep you focused and your actions will inspire others. And your purpose statement defines your *why* from this point forward

- The external-facing brand attributes: experiences, presence, and description reflect how you show up. Others define the authenticity of your brand based on the experiences they have with you. Your presence in person and on social media create a picture of who you are and what you care about. The way others describe you is a clue. It's a way to step outside yourself and hear how others articulate who you are from their perspective. Only you can determine if they got it right or if you need to course correct so your external brand attributes match your inner motivations and what matters to you

- When authentically demonstrated, your six brand attributes will keep you facing in the direction of what matters. They become a compass pointing to your True North. But, even if your brand meets all the criteria of authenticity, it won't resonate with everyone. If you are really being true to yourself, then you are bound to resonate with some and not others. Every day you make choices about brands—business and people—based on the experiences you have with them, the way they make you feel, and how connected you feel to what they stand for. Others will do the same as it relates to your brand

**Don't try to be all things to all people. Just do you.**

# Part Three

## Your True North

# Chapter 7
# Identify Conflicts

*Have the courage to follow your heart and intuition. They somehow already know what you truly want to become.*

Steve Jobs

While reflecting on your brand authenticity, you may have discovered that you're not sharing the real you, or that what matters to you isn't evident in the experiences you're creating in some of your relationships. Perhaps you've realized that you're delivering on promises in one area of your life but falling short in others. Maybe you're using up your energy and emotions on certain people and situations, so you feel drained during other interactions.

When you're able to identify the conflicts in your personal brand, it will be easier to recognize when a person (or group of people), a job, a community, a cause, or an organization is allowing you to be your best self—to openly live your brand. If you trust your gut and align your decisions and actions with what matters to you and who you are, you'll know what's worth working toward and what's worth walking away from.

This chapter will help you identify conflicts. You'll learn:

- Why you should write your own story
- Why living your purpose will bring you joy
- When to listen to your inner voice
- Why you should care about your brand online

## Writing the Next Chapter

My son Andrew is one of those rare people who knew exactly what he wanted to do at a relatively young age. He knew he was meant to be a designer. As a child, he'd spend endless hours building masterpieces with LEGO. This creativity evolved into drawing, graphic design, and eventually a love for user experience design. His dream was to go to the Rochester Institute of Technology (RIT) and study new media design. We visited the campus and he was instantly sold. He didn't even want to consider any other schools. His mind was made up and he was accepted. He was ecstatic!

Andrew's drive and decisiveness has always impressed me. When he commits to doing something, he does it. He puts in the time and work to achieve what he wants. Unfortunately, he found himself in a difficult situation when his high school girlfriend wanted him to go to the school at which she'd been accepted. Andrew, a self-sacrificing young man who never wants to let people down, struggled under the pressure she put on him to alter his plans.

One night, she drove off in her car after threatening to harm herself if my son didn't change his mind. We immediately called the police, fearful she'd get in an accident. The police found her and brought her home to her parents. She was furious with my son because she didn't want her parents to know about her behavior.

For me, the decision seemed obvious: Andrew should chase his dream. If the relationship was meant to be, it would last through college.

But Andrew found it difficult to navigate the pressure from his girlfriend. It was heart-wrenching to watch him go through this, and we spent many hours discussing it. Once he was able to separate himself from the emotional storm and refocus his energy on his dream, he decided to go to RIT regardless of the fallout with his girlfriend. As it turned out, the relationship didn't last long into the summer before college. But as anticipated, Andrew loved his time at RIT, made great friends, and landed a terrific job prior to graduation. Plus, he met and fell in love with a wonderful young woman, Jill, who loves him for exactly who he is. They support each other's dreams and make decisions about the future together.

Needless to say, I'm pleased and proud that Andrew wrote the next chapter of his story and stayed true to himself and his dreams. At a young age, he learned the importance of surrounding himself with people who recognize and support his dreams and talents. He learned that people who are willing to manipulate to get others to do what they want should be written out of the story.

## Your Next Chapter

The opportunity to take control and write the next chapter in the story of your life is yours for the taking. Maybe there are people or things you want to write *out* of the next chapter of your story. Or perhaps you yearn to write something meaningful *into* your next chapter. To identify these things, revisit the personal brand authenticity charts in Chapter 6. Look at the areas where your scores are lower and ask yourself, "What's getting in my way?" Then look at the areas where you gave yourself high scores and consider why this might be the case. Is it a matter of greater support or commitment? What factors are allowing you to behave consistently in some areas and not others?

If you're truly committed to living your brand, your new self-awareness will become your True North, your internal compass leading you and keeping you focused. It may be difficult, but it's important to acknowledge if any of your relationships, personal or professional, are leading you away from your True North. If you're honest with yourself, you may see that you're making choices that make you uncomfortable in order to meet someone else's expectations. Maybe some of these expectations conflict with your values. Pay attention to anything that makes you pause or feel ill at ease.

Reflect on your purpose statement and determine whether you're working toward it. It may feel overwhelming to take it on at this point in your life, but to find joy, you have to put a stake in the ground and declare who you are, what you stand for, and what you aim to achieve.

## A Purpose-Filled Life

Unlike my son, my daughter was uncertain about what she wanted to do with her life when she was in high school. After much thought, Jessica elected to attend a local community college and study liberal arts. She also wanted to get some work experience, so she took a sales job at T-Mobile. She became an expert on mobile phones and quickly became a top-performing sales associate. Her outgoing, bubbly personality served her well.

Even as a part-time employee, Jessica got noticed—she was offered the opportunity to go through management training. Her leaders felt she had a bright career in retail. But, even as her income and success grew, she didn't feel any connection to the work. She realized that she didn't want to pursue a career in retail or sales.

Seemingly out of the blue, she announced that she wanted to volunteer at a local children's psychiatric hospital. She'd always been interested in psychology and decided it was time she explored that field. Jessica jumps into things headfirst—I admire that about her. Her experiences with the children at the psychiatric hospital ended up being life changing. Jessica discovered her purpose. She became passionate about doing her part to help others.

From that point forward, Jessica shifted her focus to social work. She earned a master's degree in human services and has a great job at a large hospital. She's living her purpose every day. The work is hard and often heartbreaking, but she knows she's making a difference one life at a time. Knowing this brings her great joy. Jessica is a powerful, outspoken advocate for her patients.

When I asked her why being a social worker mattered so much to her, she replied, "We can allow our experiences to shape us and teach us something, or we can let them consume us. I believe it's a choice, and being a social worker gives me the opportunity to show others that they have that choice. Let's be honest—social work isn't a glamorous job. I see people at their lowest points, in some of the worst living conditions, after experiencing trauma or making one decision that changed the trajectory of their entire lives. Even though I've seen a lot of ugly, I still choose to believe that the world is a beautiful place. If I can make a positive impact on someone's life, even if it's only making one dark moment easier to bear, that means I've done my job. I love helping people realize how resilient they are."

You have defined your purpose. The question to ask yourself is whether you feel empowered to go after it. If the answer is no, consider why that is. What's holding you back? If the barriers are time or financial constraints, the best approach is to create a plan to fulfill your purpose over time. Go back to your responses to the career and aspirations questions in Chapter 2 and get more specific about your plan. When you write down your goals with clear, actionable steps, they become real. Put milestones on your calendar to hold yourself accountable.

Your purpose may be aligned with the field you're currently in. Or fulfilling it may require significant change. Either way, creating a roadmap and holding yourself accountable is the way to achieve what you desire and find joy in your life's work.

## Trust Your Gut

Don't ignore your inner voice. At various times in your life, you've likely suppressed it in order to cope with something, perhaps a stressful or toxic situation. Maybe you felt the situation was a *means to an end* or a *necessary evil.* Whatever phrase you assigned to the way you were feeling and its related experiences, it was simply a label to mask what was really going on. Your inner voice was telling you that you were off course. Something wasn't in sync with some aspect of what matters to you.

This inner voice is shaped by your past experiences and the knowledge you've gained from them. Researchers say it's an elaborate warning system.[1]

At one point in my career, I chose to leave a stable job to join a company that offered an opportunity to learn and grow. A new challenge was exactly what I was seeking at that stage of my career—or so I thought.

Before the company made me an offer, I had a few meetings with the CEO and executive vice president, which went well. I was flattered and excited each time I spoke with them, but I also felt something I couldn't quite put my finger on.

Ultimately, I ignored that little voice inside me—disregarding it as fear or remorse for leaving a company and people I loved—and took the leap. After all, the offer was good, the company had an enviable customer base, and I'd be able to develop many new skills.

For the first few months, I went to work every day wearing my rose-colored glasses and putting in imaginary earplugs to drown out my inner voice. But as time went on, I realized that I'd sacrificed many of the things that really mattered to me in order to take this job. I'd put growth and learning ahead of some of the *most* important things, such as authentic leadership, collaborative peer relationships, and a culture focused on developing people. My inner voice screamed as I began to see the company for what it was. The stories I'd been told during the interview process weren't at all representative of the culture or the leadership. As a result, the work didn't resonate with me.

But I'd told my friends and family it was a great decision, so my pride stood in the way for a while. I was too ashamed to admit I'd made a terrible mistake. I'd known it was time to move on from my previous job, but I'd come to this new company for all the wrong reasons. The stress and anxiety of this reality began to manifest in ways I couldn't have anticipated. I had migraines often, and I wasn't mentally present during family functions—I was always worrying about work and trying to keep up a good front. My energy was low, and I wasn't making time for workouts or running (which are critical to my well-being).

When I finally admitted to my husband how I was really feeling, a huge weight was lifted. I hit the reset button and revisited my list of what matters. I embraced being the outlier and focused my energy on being the best leader I could be in that role for my team. But most importantly, I started listening to my inner voice again and ultimately left the company. Leaving was one of the best career decisions I've ever made.

Listening to your gut is important to your overall health and well-being. Your brain is always searching the databank of your experiences and sending up red flags when necessary. Be willing to consider them.

## Your Brand Online

If you answered "Yes!" to the question in Chapter 5, *See Who Others See*, "Is there anyone in my personal or professional life whom I would NOT want to see some of my social media activity?" you need to work on your online profiles. You might have immediately thought of a parent—maybe you don't want them to see your pictures from an event in which you conducted yourself in a way they wouldn't approve of. Or maybe you thought of Grandma and that meme, joke, or story that was best left to a private message. Even if you didn't send it, if you liked or shared it, you're complicit.

If you thought of your leaders or colleagues but assumed that employers and potential employers aren't really interested in what you post, think again. Seeking to find and retain employees who fit their culture and represent the company brand, employers are digging deeper into social media to learn as much as they can.[2]

Another important thing to consider is the movement toward a gig economy. More and more people are seeking contract or freelance jobs.[3] If you're a freelancer, you and your social media profiles *are* your brand. Be sure that you represent your brand professionally.

Let's compare and contrast two people I'll call Connie and Steve. They are both millennials who were in the process of changing jobs when they sought my advice about how to identify the next right step in their careers.

Connie had been with her company for six years. Although her responsibilities grew, her salary remained stagnant and she was feeling like there wasn't a clear career path. She had spoken to her manager, who offered little guidance about expanding her role. Connie was feeling disengaged and realized it was time to pursue something else. She was strong in sales and really enjoyed working with people. So, she started reaching out to other organizations and applying for sales roles. She wasn't getting any responses and became worried. When she approached me and shared her situation, we looked at her social media presence and it became clear that she was not representing her brand effectively.

Connie hadn't ever created a LinkedIn profile or sought professional recommendations. She was nearly invisible on LinkedIn. Her Facebook and Instagram pages were full of pictures of her favorite meals and paired alcoholic beverages. Professionally, she was nonexistent online. If prospective employers sought to learn more about Connie, they might surmise that she enjoys good food and drink—but would she be a good salesperson? Connie had a lot of work to do to become more relevant online. She realized that she was not representing her passion for her work. After updating her professional profile, within a few months she began hearing from recruiters regarding sales positions.

Steve had worked for two companies. He had a terrific experience in his first company and left on good terms for another opportunity with a larger company. Upon his departure, he asked his leader, his peers, and a few customers to write recommendations on LinkedIn. Steve had carefully crafted his LinkedIn profile with his education, work experience, and actively followed other companies and leaders who inspired him. During his time at the second company, he realized that the work didn't resonate with him. He began to recognize another purpose for his work life and wanted to pursue it. Steve sought my advice as he considered options for the next step in his career. He knew he needed to be discerning so he could redirect his efforts to fulfill his purpose.

In preparation, Steve updated his resume and his LinkedIn profile to reflect all he had learned and accomplished. He worked hard to maintain the professional relationships at his company, knowing that their recommendations would be important as he moved on in his career—he didn't want to burn any bridges. Because of his profile and activity on LinkedIn, Steve was frequently hearing from recruiters. This allowed him to consider options and select what was right for him. Prospective employers could get a sense of who Steve was based on his professional profile. On his other social media pages, he shared pictures of his travels, his daughter, races he was running, and family gatherings. It was pretty easy to glimpse into his world and get a sense of Steve and what mattered to him.

Steve and Connie were at about the same level professionally but clearly Steve was much more prepared to make a career move. Connie was at a disadvantage because she didn't think about her online brand until she really needed to change jobs. Steve had carefully tended to his online presence and appeared to be clearer about his priorities, and as a result, was more desirable to prospective employers. That became evident based on the number of recruiters who reached out to Steve versus Connie.

## Identify Conflicts: Summary

You're the author of your story. Examine what you want to write into it and what should be written out, so you stay focused on your True North.

Create a plan that holds you accountable to your purpose and outlines the steps you need to take to get there. Living your purpose will bring you joy.

Listen to your inner voice and trust yourself. You know yourself best and your past experiences offer lessons that can guide you as you make decisions today.

Finally, be intentional when it comes to your online brand. Who you are online matters to your personal and professional relationships. It's an expression of who you are and what matters to you, so make sure it's working to build your brand, not damage it.

## Chapter 8

# When Life Derails Your Brand

*Your inner knowing is your only true compass.*

Joy Page

Life will throw you curveballs. It will test you. When you have a clear picture of yourself and something unexpected changes that picture, it can shake you to the core.

People tend to lose their sense of self when catastrophe strikes, such as being diagnosed with a life-threatening illness, losing a loved one, getting fired from a job, being in an accident, or ending a relationship. Catastrophes force us to face a new part of our brand—a part we might not necessarily want to face.

In this chapter, you will learn:

- How to navigate your way back to your True North when you're thrown off course
- The importance of separating events from people

## My Plan

My parents were high school sweethearts. They met in tenth grade and were together nearly every day until my mother's death at the young age of seventy-two. The example they set for my sisters and me was one of lifelong love and dedication. Growing up, I couldn't picture any better example of marriage and what I should strive for. In fact, even though it was never really discussed, I always felt I was *supposed* to meet my lifelong love in high school—that is, if I wanted to recreate what my parents had.

When I started dating my high school sweetheart in eleventh grade, I thought destiny had a firm grasp on my life. Although we had a few on-again-off-again phases, he declared his undying love for me during my senior year, and I was overjoyed. The night of my senior prom, he surprised me with a diamond ring and proposed. I thought, *This is exactly the way it's meant to be.* When I think about that magical night, I can't believe how young and naïve we were—he in a white tux and I in a big poof-y blue dress and eighties updo, announcing to all our friends that we were going to get married.

You see, I'm a planner. I can see that planner mentality playing out across my entire life. I always have a plan for the future with short-term and long-term goals and a vision of how to achieve them. At the time of my high school graduation, my plan was to be a civil engineer and to marry my high school sweetheart. Although I wouldn't have used branding language at that time in my life, I would have defined my brand using those descriptors. I felt that the end of high school was the beginning of life and I needed to take charge. So, I did.

But things don't always go as planned. Circumstances change, people change, and plans change. Later, when I was six months pregnant with my daughter, I learned that the man I'd thought I'd spend the rest of my life with had been unfaithful. And I was also beginning to suspect that he had an alcohol problem and that I'd been in deep denial. When confronted, he declared that he wouldn't stop drinking and didn't intend to stop seeing the other woman. It was over.

Ashamed and disillusioned, I had to go home to my parents, tell them the horror of the situation, and ask for their help. I felt I'd completely failed at everything. I was someone I was never supposed to be—a soon-to-be single mother who had to depend on her parents for support. My entire world was rocked to its core. If I was none of the things I'd set out to be, who was I? My life had been abruptly redefined for me without my permission. I didn't want the new labels that came with my unintended circumstances.

As I reflect on that time with the benefit of years of experience and gained wisdom, I realize that I was so wrapped up in creating what my parents had that I didn't really think about whether I truly loved the father of my daughter. I thought I did at the time, but I think what I really loved was the idea of finding lifelong love. I was naïvely willing to link my identity to him without fully understanding who he was. My daughter was the greatest gift I received from that experience. She's an amazing person and one of the very best things that has ever come into my life.

It wasn't until I embraced my new identity that I was able to move past the pain, anger, and shame that followed this disruption in my life. My coping mechanism has always been to learn from and analyze situations. In an effort to prevent future mistakes and create the best possible life for my daughter, I immersed myself in everything I could related to alcoholism. I even attended Al-Anon meetings to better understand alcoholism and drug addiction. I learned a great deal, made wonderful friends, and grew so much through the experience.

I also set my focus on my career and becoming exactly what I felt I was meant to be professionally. I believed I had something to prove to the world. I had much to overcome and didn't want to face the biases that come with being a young single mother. Nor did I want people to look at my daughter with pity because her father had chosen not to play a role in her life. She and I were a team, and I was determined to show her what strength and perseverance looked like. I wanted to control what I could. The best I could do for both me and my daughter was to commit to being my best self.

I wasn't really open to a new relationship when a man at work asked me out. I knew Bill King, but not well. I somewhat reluctantly agreed, worried about dating a colleague in case things went poorly. During our date, I learned that he had two sons, and I shared stories and pictures of my daughter. We talked and laughed for hours. The first date went so well that he asked to take me out again the following weekend, which happened to be my birthday. A few short months into our relationship, we both knew that we'd found what we were looking for. We'd just attended a conference where the theme was Bold Goals, and Bill asked me what mine were. Not sensing where he was going with the question, I replied with something work related and then asked him the same question. Bill replied, "To marry you!"

Bill and I were married on January 25, 1992. We have built a *yours, mine, and ours* blended family that we're incredibly proud of. Bill's two boys, Tim and Brian, were the most welcoming big brothers to my daughter Jessica. I love them dearly and am so grateful that I've been a part of their lives. Bill adopted Jessica and has been the best father she and I could have hoped for. Then, in 1994, our son Andrew was born. From the moment Andrew came into the world, our life has had more excitement, humor, and joy. Andrew has an infectious energy and spark. Our life is full and happy. In Bill, I found my soulmate. Instead of being married to my high school sweetheart, I'm married to an older man and I'm exactly who I'm supposed to be. My brand is different.

Unforeseen circumstances and disrupted plans proved to be opportunities for me to discover my authentic self. If my experiences had been different early in my adult life, I might not care as much about paying it forward in my life's work now. Maybe I wouldn't have been as moved to see young leaders on my team accomplish more than they thought was possible. Maybe I would have taken for granted the amazing mentors, luck, and opportunities I had early in my career. Instead, I saw these as precious gifts. My life lessons and shifting paths have shaped me. They've given me opportunities to define what matters to me. I wouldn't change one single thing.

## Returning to Your True North

We all know people who've been dealt a difficult blow—people in situations that have forced them to reevaluate what matters and define or redefine their life's purpose.

I know a young mother whose child was diagnosed with cancer. She left her job and dedicated her life to caring for her son. Her career no longer mattered. A new purpose emerged. She learned everything she could about his cancer and became a passionate advocate for him and other kids suffering from the same illness.

I know a baby boomer who was downsized and forced to reinvent himself. He needed to explore what he wanted to do in the next phase of his life, after decades with the same company. He'd never thought about what mattered to him, and although it was scary, he found the opportunity liberating. For the first time in his life, he allowed himself to consider what *his* purpose was. He leveraged his expertise and vast network and started his own business.

I know a millennial who wanted to be a chef. Her parents pressured her to go to business school, convincing her that she wouldn't be happy working in a kitchen. After incurring debt and getting a good job at a large company, she realized she was miserable and felt stuck. She wasn't living *her* dream. Slowly, she built a business on the side that started with a blog about vegan recipes. Then, she began cooking and baking for small functions. Her business is growing, and her dream is becoming her reality.

When life derails you, it's critical to reevaluate what matters to you. Then reconnect your authentic brand attributes to what matters so you can find your True North in the storm. Some of the things you previously identified as important may shift as a result of a new and necessary focus. This new focus may reignite your purpose, or it may create a new purpose. Be open to the possibilities and know that your brand will always grow as you learn through life experiences.

## You are Not the Event

It's also important to separate yourself from the event that changed things. For instance, the boomer who lost his job struggled with the shift in his identity—he went from being an executive for most of his adult life to being unemployed, and he was ashamed. It wasn't until he was able to separate himself from the event and reestablish his brand identity as someone who wasn't an employee that he was able to move forward.

When you encounter a situation that's out of your control, ask yourself if your actions caused the event. Is there anything you could have done to prevent it? The mere fact that the event was out of your control suggests that you couldn't have done anything differently. But, if there was something you could have done, recognize that you are human, and mistakes happen. Learn from the situation and accept that it does not need to define you. Allow yourself to visualize the separation of the event from you as a person. There is what happened, and then there is who you are. Who you are doesn't change. You may need to shift your focus to adapt to your new circumstances, but your values, the authentic you can rise to the occasion during these difficult times. This is where you'll have the opportunity to shine as a leader.

## Own Your New Description

Your new circumstances may require you to update your description. This is a chance for you to take control of the narrative and help others understand more about this shift in your brand. The young mother whose son had cancer left a job as a director at an advertising agency and became a passionate advocate for children with cancer. The boomer who was laid off became an entrepreneur. The millennial who was working in a large company became a popular blogger and chef.

When I elected to leave the corporate world and start a business, people gave me befuddled looks when I explained what I was doing. This was a decision I'd made, not something that had happened *to* me.

Some people were inspired and felt I was bold to throw caution to the wind and pursue my purpose. Others were stunned that I was willing to give up my stable job to take on the risk of a start-up—at my age! I had a career as an executive in marketing and branding, and people who knew me could describe who I was and what I did. Now, I was an anomaly. They didn't know what to say about me. I took the opportunity to craft my new description:

> *I am an entrepreneur who leverages my marketing, branding, and leadership experience to energize and empower the next generation of leaders to live their brand and lead with authenticity and purpose.*

## When Life Derails Your Brand: Summary

Remaining authentic and living your brand will always see you through the storm. The exercises in this book are the tools you need to navigate the planned and unplanned changes in your life.

You can revisit the exercises at any time, capture your responses, and modify your purpose and promises as needed. After all, you'll continue to experience more profound moments that teach you valuable life lessons. Your Venn diagram, containing what matters to you, can always be reworked. The power and authenticity of your brand will be tested at some point in your life, but your ability to navigate the storm and stay true to you will keep you focused on your True North.

In Part Four, *Your Time to Lead*, I'll provide examples of what matters in leadership and challenge you to tap into the power of your unique strengths.

# Key Takeaways, Part Three

## YOUR TRUE NORTH

- There are elements of your brand that you *can* control, such as what's written into or out of the next chapter of your story. Making changes may be difficult, but you need to take action when your personal or professional relationships aren't aligned with your True North

- You also control your brand online. Who you are online and how you're perceived by those who matter most to you is tied directly to your brand. Make sure you're expressing who you are and what you value

- Trust your gut. When your inner voice is trying to tell you something, listen. When you listen, you'll begin to see more clearly what's aligned with your purpose and principles and what's not

- When something comes your way that you don't expect or cannot control, separate *you* the person from the *event*. Once you do that, you can proceed with a plan to work through the situation. If you stay mired in the muck of your new circumstances and attach them to your brand, you'll lose your focus on your True North

- If you encounter a major change in your life and it forces you to rethink what matters, go back to the exercises in this book to reestablish your purpose, promises, and principles. Update your Venn diagram according to what matters to you personally, professionally, and aspirationaly. Define the experiences you wish to create. And update your description so that it contains the full expression of who you are and how you want others to see you, regardless of whether the change was planned or unplanned.

**Through the storm, an authentic leader will emerge stronger.**

# Part Four

## Your Time to Lead

## Chapter 9

# What Matters in Leadership

> *And when we feel sure they will keep us safe we will march behind them and work tirelessly to see their visions come to life and proudly call ourselves their followers.*
>
> Simon Sinek

Now that you have a clear picture of your brand, it matters that you start living and leading with authenticity and purpose. It matters that you acknowledge those times in your life when you stepped up and led. It matters that you realize when you've missed the opportunity to lead because you didn't feel it was your place. It matters that you forgive yourself for any leadership mishaps in the past and move forward. It matters that you lead as your authentic self. It matters that you try, even if you think you aren't ready. It matters that you step forward to fill the leadership gap. It matters that you become the leader you wish you had. It matters that you inspire others to dream more, learn more, do more, and become more.

In this chapter, I'll share stories of leadership from my own experiences as well as from others. Through this journey, I hope that you've opened your mind and perhaps rethought what you believe to be true about authentic leadership. It's not about title, position, or power.

You'll see that authentic leaders:

- Lead by example
- Take leaps of faith and are willing to learn
- Fail forward and lead others through failure
- Take ownership and responsibility
- Are willing to be outliers
- Understand how their actions affect others

I'll explain how the leadership behaviors in the following stories have helped shape or challenge brand attributes. Each story is followed by the brand authenticity summary, which illustrates the resulting personal development that came from the experience.

## Lead by Example

You can be a leader at any age and develop your leadership skills over time. Successful leaders are defined by their character, not their title. When leaders are authentic, they motivate and encourage others to become leaders themselves. Often, we don't realize the impact we have on those around us until someone lets us know.

As we've previously covered, leadership experiences happen in all aspects of life—not just at work. When you live your life in a way that positively affects others, you set an example and give them permission to do the same.

One of the highest compliments I've ever received came from Tom Denari, president and chief strategy officer at Young & Laramore, an agency I hired and worked with for many years. When Tom wrote a recommendation on my LinkedIn profile, he described me this way: "When I reflect on the times that I worked with Lisa

King, both at Galyans and Raymour & Flanigan, what struck me the most was that she was always the calmest person in the room. She was unflappable. No matter how difficult or unwieldy the situation, Lisa displayed a quiet confidence and grace that is uncommon these days." Up until that point in my career, I hadn't really thought about the fact that I set an example of calm. I was humbled by his words and realized that this was an important attribute of my personal brand.

As a leader of large teams, I've always felt it was my responsibility to assess each situation and rally the troops to tackle the challenge at hand. For me, it's a natural response to stress. I just hadn't realized that this intuitive approach was recognized and valued by those around me. Upon reflection, I know I despised it when other leaders blew up in times of stress. I could see everyone around them cower. I never wanted to create that kind of atmosphere. I wanted to set an example of calm so others would see that a solution was possible if we worked together.

Over the years, I've heard comments similar to Tom's from my team, my peers, and my leaders. They've appreciated my example and told me about times when my calm approach helped them navigate a difficult situation. Mission accomplished.

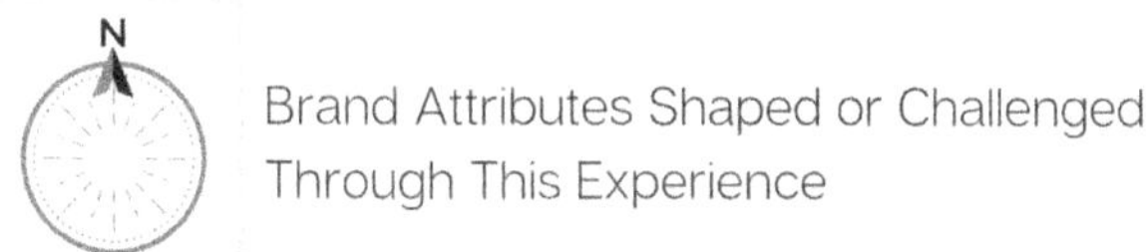


- I keep my *promises:* I commit to remaining calm in a storm
- I adhere to my *principles:* I care for those in my charge
- I provide *experiences* that are consistently fulfilling: My team can expect me to rationally approach a situation
- I have a *presence* that's genuine: I bring the right energy and emotion to the situation
- My brand matches the *description* others give it: I'm described as calm and confident in a variety of situations

When asked to reflect on a time when she led by example, Jenna shared the following story.

Jenna

*"High school was difficult for me. I wasn't quite sure where I fit in. I played sports, I was in band, I was shy and a bit awkward but at the same time I could be loud and obnoxious. My favorite class was art because I was able to express myself though my creativity. In my final class, I was given a pink envelope with my name on it from a quiet girl with whom I'd had very few interactions. In the envelope was a thank-you card that read, "Thank you for showing me that it's okay to be yourself no matter what others think. I'll sing loudly and dance on top of the table if it makes me happy." Prior to that, I hadn't realized that I'd had any kind of impact on her. Upon reflection, I realized that I was transparent and honest in my actions, and that resonated with her. At first, seeing how my actions could affect another person was intimidating, but now it's absolutely empowering."*

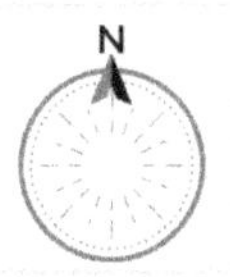


Brand Attributes Shaped or Challenged Through This Experience

- She adheres to her *principles:* Jenna did this even when it seemed no one is looking
- She provides *experiences* that are consistently fulfilling: Trust was built, and the girl felt comfortable enough to send a thank-you note to Jenna even though she didn't know her well
- She has a *presence* that's genuine: Jenna expressed herself through her art and was seen as authentic

## Take Leaps of Faith and Be Willing to Learn

Sometimes, leadership is about being vulnerable. Taking on something new requires commitment and a plan. It's important to define what you want to learn or need to know to be successful. Don't be afraid to seek advice from a mentor, take a class, get training through your company, research a topic or skill, or learn by doing. There are bound to be twists and turns on your learning journey, but if you remain open-minded, you'll have a greater chance of success. And remember, you own your mind. You don't need permission from anyone to grow and expand.

In the late 1980s, about a year after I started my job at Dick's Sporting Goods, I was approached by the CEO, Ed. He asked me if I thought I could lead the effort to bring our marketing in-house. At the time, an agency was doing our television, radio, and newspaper advertising. My mind raced and terror surged inside me. I was still taking college classes at night and on weekends. I didn't feel ready. But I was managing all in-store sign production, and though I had no staff reporting directly to me, I was successfully collaborating with all departments and stores, which he'd noticed. It occurred to me that if I said no, I'd be missing a huge opportunity that might not come along again. I gathered my composure and said, "Yes, I can put together a plan to bring marketing in-house."

Ed replied, "Great, I look forward to seeing it—soon!"

After he left, I immediately went to see my leader and mentor, Bill. He encouraged me to put the draft of the plan together and offered to review it before I shared it with the CEO. You see, Bill had more confidence in my strengths than I did at the time. He planted seeds with Ed about my capabilities and worked to create opportunities for me based on his belief in me.

*I think the biggest opportunity as a leader is to get your team comfortable with stretching, failing, and learning. If leaders can do that, then anything is possible. I hope that I helped people see what they are capable of and truly believe in themselves. Then, maybe they will take that forward and do that for other people as well.*

Bill Colombo, Dick's Sporting Goods vice-chairman of the board, former president and COO

I created two plans, each of which covered staffing, systems, and a budget for the new in-house marketing department. One was conservative and the other was more aggressive. Bill carefully looked them both over, held up the conservative one, and, with a smile on his face, tore it up in front of me. Then he held up the aggressive plan and said, "This is what you're presenting." I felt a rush of adrenaline. I was determined to succeed and not let Bill down. I presented the plan, got the approval, and my marketing career began.

I realize that luck and opportunity collided for me at Dick's Sporting Goods. But I also took a leap of faith and worked hard to realize my dreams. I was fortunate to have Bill there to create opportunities for me and help build my confidence. The lessons I learned from Bill and through all my years at Dick's were invaluable. I'm grateful to this day for the chance that was taken on me way back then. I wouldn't be the person or leader I am today had I not taken initiative and had Bill as a mentor.

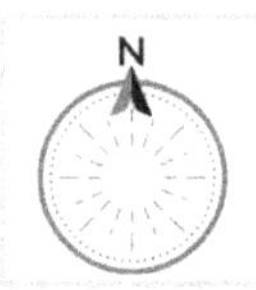


Brand Attributes Shaped or Challenged Through This Experience

- I keep my *promises:* I was determined to succeed and delivered on my commitment to build the department
- I adhere to my *principles:* I take care of those in my charge and those who lead me
- I provide *experiences* that are consistently fulfilling: Based on his experiences with me, Bill had more confidence in me than I did in myself; his confidence fueled me.

When asked to reflect on a time when she took a leap of faith and grew as a leader, Nicole shared the following story.

Nicole

*"My small start-up business was growing, and I hired five part-time employees. I had no prior leadership experience, but I was passionate about my business and I shared that passion with my employees. I had to train them on how to produce our product and maintain a pace to keep up with customer demand. At first it was intimidating to teach people both older and younger than me. But I gave them all the time they needed, answered their questions, and did my best to ensure they had all the tools they needed to do their jobs. They followed my advice and it made me feel like I knew what I was doing—like I could lead! I really enjoyed the experience of teaching others a new skill and seeing them become interested in the business I was creating."*

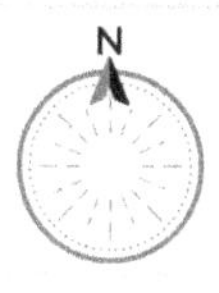


Brand Attributes Shaped or Challenged Through This Experience

- She has a clear *purpose:* Nicole showed her passion and let employees know what the business stood for
- She keeps her *promises:* She was committed to answering questions and allowed time for employees to learn
- She adheres to her *principles:* Nicole demonstrated patience with employees and passion for a job well done
- She provides *experiences* that are consistently fulfilling: Employees learned and Nicole grew as a leader
- She has a *presence* that's genuine: Employees knew Nicole was a new leader and they respected her willingness to learn alongside them

## Allow Yourself to Fail Forward and Lead Others Through Failure

As a leader, you can observe and learn from everyone around you. Make mental notes of what you learn from both good and bad leaders. The lessons are equally important. I've learned as much from bad leaders as I have from good ones. The bad ones reinforce what I don't want to be like and help solidify my core principles.

Don't get me wrong—I've failed as much as I've succeeded. I've made mistakes and fallen short as a leader. Mistakes and failures can be some of the most difficult things to overcome in life. We don't always deal with them in effective ways, and we can be really hard on ourselves. But in order to move forward as leaders, we need to forgive those who have wronged us and forgive ourselves.

Mistakes happen. We're all human. Things will go wrong in business and people will fall down sometimes. How a leader reacts in these times of stress will determine how employees behave. There's valuable learning to be had if the leader invites employees to be honest and talk about what happened. Leaders can also gain great respect from employees if they take responsibility for their own mistakes. It's not a sign of weakness—it actually strengthens the organization. Employees see the leader as human, and this builds a relationship of mutual trust. In a trusting environment, employees are more willing to share failures as well as successes.

Joan, one of the great leaders I had the privilege of working with, was open and honest with her team about failures. She admitted when one of her ideas or something she was responsible for didn't go as planned. Joan used these experiences as opportunities to brainstorm with her team of executives, and each of us grew individually as a result. We also grew stronger as a team. We felt confident proposing innovative, risky solutions. Our exchange of experiences and ideas drove fresh thinking. It led to effective problem-solving and better cross-functional collaboration.

A culture without trust is a culture driven by fear and insecurity—a culture of people who want to hide their mistakes. They may not be willing to seek innovative solutions or take risks.

One of the least effective leaders I worked with didn't lead. He bossed. I'll call him Pat. Pat's style was to knock down employees when mistakes occurred. He never took responsibility for failures, even if they were a result of employees following his direction. Consequently, many employees cowered and avoided him, interacting only when absolutely necessary. And Pat didn't know everything that was happening in the organization. Employees didn't respect or trust him —a dangerous situation for any leader. Progress stalled and employees played it safe. They were disengaged.

I found myself choosing a different path back to my desk if I saw Pat in the hallway. I avoided eye contact in meetings because I knew he would criticize my work and be unwilling to have a rational conversation about any challenges I might be facing. I feared failure and sought perfection in my projects to avoid his wrath. This drive for perfection caused me to work and rework my projects until I lost sight of what I was really working toward. I was stressed out and exhausted.

Once I realized what I was doing, I took a step back and decided that I wouldn't allow Pat's controlling, negative leadership to affect me any longer. I realized that it wasn't about me—he behaved that way with everyone. It wasn't personal. The problem was his, not mine. I made a conscious effort to communicate with confidence in meetings and to not let Pat make me question my efforts or commitment to a successful project. I knew who I was and what I stood for. Pat wouldn't make me feel like a failure.

- I have a clear *purpose:* I wasn't leading by example; I was avoiding Pat
- I keep my *promises:* I believe in open communication and transparency with my leaders, and in this situation, I was failing to be open and transparent; I needed to change that, regardless of the consequences

- I adhere to my *principles:* By avoiding Pat, I wasn't as honest as I should have been
- I provide *experiences* that are consistently fulfilling: I was overwhelmed and stressed out, striving for perfection and not doing my best work as a result
- I have a *presence* that's genuine: I didn't bring the right energy and emotion to the situation until I hit reset and decided not to take Pat's behavior personally

Beth

*"I was impacted to my core by my boss's mistrust and controlling micromanagement. I took it all personally. I couldn't understand what I was doing wrong. I thought that if I could be the leader he wanted, I could win his trust and support. It actually got worse—much worse. My team didn't understand who I was any longer. I began to micromanage my team because he required me to know ALL the details. I was short. I wasn't always kind. I lacked patience. I was too busy for anything personal, and honestly, I'd lost the capacity to be personal—it was too hard. I couldn't give direction because I was constantly being given multiple directions—I questioned everything. I wasn't living in alignment with my core values any longer. Not only was I struggling with my team, I was struggling with my son, which was impacting his behavior at home and at school. I stopped putting in the extra effort at work, because, what was the point? Then I realized life is too short. I could no longer live outside of my values and be healthy. No one should have that kind of control over my life. Staying somewhere working for someone who treats you like you're replaceable and doesn't have your back isn't worth the cost. You pay at home, you pay with your team, you pay with your soul. I made mistakes, I owned them, I beat myself up over them. I only hope my former team will eventually forgive me."*

- She adheres to her *principles:* when Beth no longer recognized herself and wasn't living in a manner consistent with her principles, she made a change
- She provides *experiences* that are consistently fulfilling: Beth realized she became a different person in order to cope with the stress; she decided to refocus on what matters
- She has a *presence* that's genuine: Beth yearned to get back to who she really was and knew that was the key to personal and professional happiness

## Take Ownership and Responsibility

There comes a point in everyone's leadership journey where there is no guide. You encounter a situation or obstacle that tests your leadership skills. It's easy to expect someone else to solve things: your boss, a colleague, a friend. But this is an opportunity to take ownership and grow. Don't wait for someone to jump in on your behalf. Jump in yourself and lead the way through it. The benefit will be far greater and the lesson that much sweeter if you get there on your own.

Several years ago, when I was a vice president at Galyan's, a dynamic, growing retail organization, I learned a valuable lesson that would dramatically change the expectations I had of my leader. The retailer was on the verge of going public and the parent company had recently hired a new chief marketing officer, Edward. I was eager to establish credibility with Edward and get him up to speed on our marketing strategy, media plan, and my staff's outstanding efforts. We had several meetings, and it seemed things were going well. I came prepared to each meeting with all the necessary materials and easily answered all his questions.

A few weeks later, after Edward felt more familiar with our overall marketing strategy, he asked me to set up a meeting with everyone from the marketing and merchandising departments. I quickly agreed, sent out the invites, and set up the room classroom style for over fifty people. Two of the other marketing leaders and I sat at a table in the front of the room with an empty seat left for Edward. He strolled into the meeting ten minutes late, saying hello to people by name and cracking jokes. The energy in the room was immediately elevated. Edward clearly had the group's attention. Then he sat down next to me, leaned over, and whispered, "What is this meeting about?"

I froze. I'd expected *him* to define the purpose of the meeting and present his brilliant vision to the room full of eager listeners. I replied, "Um . . . I'm not sure. You just asked that I set it up."

Quick on his feet, he turned to the audience, made a few introductory remarks, and then said, "I'd like to take this opportunity to have Lisa walk you all through our marketing strategy." Several emotions raced through me, but mostly shock and a feeling of being very underprepared. Normally, I run meetings thoroughly prepared with an agenda, a compelling presentation, and takeaways. Instead, I sat with a blank notebook in front of me, mouth agape. All eyes in the room were on me. I gathered my composure, reminded myself that I was clearly the most knowledgeable person in the room regarding our current marketing strategy, and launched into an overview. I left the meeting disillusioned and angry. My expectations of Edward were shattered.

I simmered in my anger for a bit, and then the hard truth hit me. I hadn't sought to understand what Edward needed from me. It wasn't his failure—it was mine. I had a lot to learn from his strengths. He was always nimble in the moment and presented brilliantly. He knew how to capture attention. I also recognized that I could bring some structure to the meetings, prepare presentations, and move initiatives forward alongside him. I could use my strengths to support him and fill the gaps. His entrepreneurial free spirit combined with my strategic approach proved to be a winning combination.

I learned to manage upward by creating the narrative and strategy. Edward taught me to be quick on my feet and to trust my gut, as being uber prepared didn't always serve the needs of the moment.

Together, we partnered with our vendors and generated millions of dollars to support our marketing efforts.

Fast-forward many years later, I was working at Raymour & Flanigan Furniture and attending an event with a new celebrity partner, Kathy Ireland (now CEO of the global brand kathy ireland Worldwide), with whom we'd recently launched a new furniture line. In a room of over three hundred people, Kathy surprised me by asking me to come to the front of the room to say a few words. As I navigated my way to the stage to stand next to this beautiful and brilliant former supermodel and address the room, I chuckled to myself and said a private thank-you to Edward. He'd prepared me for this moment.

We often have very high expectations of our leaders. After working for Bill at Dick's, and initially Joan and Galyan's, I had an expectation that leaders should pave the way, provide crystal clear guidance, deliver strategic direction, and set me up for success. The truth is, each of us owns the responsibility for our personal success as leaders. It wasn't until I altered my expectations of myself that I was open to learning and growing in unexpected ways. Up until that point in my career, all my leaders had given me exactly what I needed. Edward's not doing so proved to be exactly what I really needed.

- I keep my *promises:* I had to revisit my commitment to lifelong learning and realize that I was missing an opportunity to learn from Edward
- I provide *experiences* that are consistently fulfilling: Once I opened myself up to learn and changed my expectations of Edward, the experience was very fulfilling
- I have a *presence* that's genuine: Initially, I didn't bring the

right energy and emotion to the situation, but when I did, it made all the difference

Todd

*"The growing pains I experienced as a young leader were guided and coached with a level of understanding and tolerance that I can only hope to emulate. My favorite experience to reflect on was when a partner in my department and I were arguing every day. We both were hard workers and very dedicated, and we needed each other to be successful—but that wasn't easy to admit. After months of back and forth and a lot of coaching from our leader, we finally locked ourselves in a room to work out our differences. After at least an hour (maybe three), we concluded that our relationship came down to trust. You cannot succeed in any environment if there's no trust. It's the foundation of any success story. I had trust issues inside and outside of work, something that isn't unique but that was hard to understand in my twenties. From that day forward, we had absolute trust in each other, and I worked harder than ever before, but had more fun as well. It solidified our part of the department and we became close friends. It took a lot to sit down in that room on that day, but it really helped me professionally and in my personal life."*

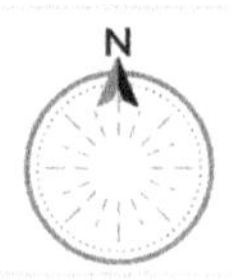


Brand Attributes Shaped or Challenged Through This Experience

- He adheres to his *principles:* Todd wanted to establish a trusting, collaborative relationship with his colleague
- He provides *experiences* that are consistently fulfilling: Camaraderie grew from that experience and the department was more successful as a result
- He has a *presence* that's genuine: Todd allowed himself to

be vulnerable to work through the differences in an effort to move forward

## Be Willing to be the Outlier

Making decisions based on your purpose and principles may not be easy. In fact, there will be times that doing so will make you an outlier. When you demonstrate leadership through authentic behavior that's aligned with what matters to you, you'll be recognized as a leader. But your decisions may not always be the popular ones. They may alienate some people. You have to decide when it's time to lead and let the chips fall where they may. I'm not suggesting leadership is about creating conflict. Rather, it's about having the courage of your convictions and respectfully expressing your position.

I moved my family from Indianapolis, Indiana, to Syracuse, New York, in 2004, as I'd accepted a great job opportunity at Raymour & Flanigan Furniture. The company was rapidly growing, and I was impressed with the owners and leaders I'd met during the interview process. Having spent my career in sporting goods retail up to this point, this was a big change, and I was excited to learn about a new industry.

The retailer was a family owned business. Second-generation owners, brothers Neil and Steve and their cousin Michael, were running the successful company. I'd been with the company for just a few weeks, focused on learning the business and understanding the current marketing strategy and budget, when Michael called me into the creative director's office to share a television commercial they'd been working on for a few months. They revealed the spot with excitement and glee while I stood there in shock. The creative director was proud of his hard work and eager to share it in an upcoming marketing meeting.

I had a very different feeling about the commercial. Although I appreciated the production value, editing, and obvious expense, I thought the commercial was a poor representation of the company and its quality. I knew I'd have to address this as soon as possible and this commercial was ready to air, according to Michael. I decided to tackle the issue later, before the next commercial was produced.

Later that day, I arrived at the marketing meeting with the owners and took my seat. I'd had little interaction with Neil and Steve up to that point. We followed the agenda and got to the dreaded moment where the creative director shared the commercial. When it ended, the room fell silent and everyone turned to look at me, the new vice president of marketing.

Neil's eyes narrowed. "What do you think, Lisa?" he said. I would come to learn that Neil, like dogs and bees, could smell fear. I cleared my throat and made the split-second decision to be brutally honest.

"I don't think the commercial adequately represents the Raymour & Flanigan brand. I understand that a lot of money was spent on this, and I'm not suggesting that we don't run it, but I recommend that we define a marketing strategy that's more aligned with the essence of the brand." As I was speaking, all I could think was that I had moved my family here, my kids had changed schools, and my home in Indianapolis was still on the market—was I about to lose my job? This was a successful company, and I'd only been here a few weeks. This "sporting goods" marketer was basically telling the owners that the commercial sucked.

After several questions from the owners, I realized that at this company, branding wasn't something that was discussed or really understood at the time. I would have to go back to basics and help the owners understand the power of branding. The meeting ended abruptly, but fortunately I wasn't fired that day. I spent ten great years at Raymour & Flanigan building the brand and delivering it through a strong marketing strategy. I had a deep conviction to deliver a brand promise that truly represented the company. That conviction drove me to be honest that day, even though it put me at risk. I believe honesty, with respect, is always the best policy.

- I keep my *promises:* I commit to doing my best and fighting for what I believe is right
- I adhere to my *principles:* It's important to me to be honest and transparent in my communications
- I have a *presence* that's genuine: Although it was difficult, I brought the right energy and emotion to the situation and was careful not to criticize the work or alienate others

### CJ

*"During my freshman year of college, one of my roommates came back from his fraternity one night and appeared to be under the influence. He was out in the hallway of our dorm messing around and ended up falling and hitting his head on the floor. He was unconscious and started to bleed slightly from his nose. My roommates and I were scared that he might have a severe injury, so I got him ice for his head. When he became conscious, he didn't want us to tell our resident advisor what happened. He thought he'd be in trouble and possibly get kicked out of the dorms or school. It appeared to me that he wasn't okay and that his need for medical attention was the priority. I got the resident advisor and we were able to get him an ambulance and safely to the hospital. Later, we found out that he had internal bleeding in his skull and a very severe concussion. If we hadn't gotten him to the hospital, he could have died. It was a very tense and scary situation, but I'm thankful I made the decision I did and was able to help my friend. Looking back at it now, I'm proud that I did what I did in the best interest of my friend, because in the long run, my decision was the right one."*

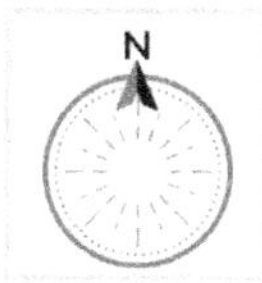


Brand Attributes Shaped or Challenged Through This Experience

- He keeps his *promises:* CJ was committed to caring for his friends and he did what was right
- He adheres to his *principles:* The value CJ placed on friendship and caring for others far outweighed his fear of getting in trouble
- He provides *experiences* that are consistently fulfilling: Through this experience, CJ demonstrated that his friends could rely on him to have their backs
- He has a *presence* that's genuine: CJ stepped up and led; he brought the right energy and emotion to the situation

## Understand How Your Leadership Affects Others

The actions of leaders have a ripple effect. And the best leaders work hard to create a positive ripple that engages and empowers those around them. Authentic leadership begins on the inside, through a deep connection to what matters and clarity regarding one's True North.

Consider the following words, which appear throughout the stories shared in this book. You'll recognize some of them from Chapter 1, *Authentic Leadership*.

### Negative Qualities in a Leader

## Results for the Followers

## Positive Qualities in a Leader

## Results for the Followers

Once you step into the light of leadership, you take on certain responsibilities, including a responsibility to be aware of your impact on your followers. What feelings do you want to evoke?

## What Matters in Leadership: Summary

You can fill the leadership gap. You now have the tools and insights to live your brand with authenticity and purpose. When you do, your influence will grow and create a positive ripple around you. You can set an example of authentic leadership–even if you are not currently experiencing it with your leaders!

Don't be afraid to take a leap of faith and learn something new. Everyone you meet and every experience you have can teach you something if you're open to learning.

We all fall down sometimes. Leaders determine whether people get knocked backward or fall forward. Encouraging the latter ignites a culture of trust and innovation.

People want to be part of a culture that embraces learning, encourages trust, and supports employees. Supporting employees through failures or mistakes doesn't mean that the leader shouldn't hold them accountable. It just means the leader understands and is extending trust. As long as the employee learns from the mistake and doesn't repeat it, they're making progress and moving forward.

As a leader, you must also be willing to be an outlier when the situation requires it. Standing up for what you believe, in a way that is respectful to others, will demonstrate your principles. When you do this, some people will take notice. They will admire your authenticity, and as a result, they may feel inspired and empowered to stand up for what they believe. That's the power of leadership.

# Chapter 10
# Your Unique Strengths

> *What will happen when we think about what is right with people rather than fixating on what is wrong with them?*
>
> Donald O. Clifton

I believe in each person's unique strengths and contributions. It's because of this belief, and my passion for developing others, that I chose to become a Gallup-certified CliftonStrengths coach.

Back in the late 1990s, Donald O. Clifton, known as the father of strengths psychology[1] and inventor of CliftonStrengths, disrupted the assessment world by challenging one major premise: he focused on improving strengths instead of fixing weaknesses. He and Gallup scientists created a common language of strengths based on decades of studies and developed the original CliftonStrengths assessment.

As a CliftonStrengths coach, I have the privilege of working with clients of all ages to create awareness of their innate talents and create development plans based on their strengths. Some of the fundamental principles of strengths-based psychology, and the benefits of creating an awareness of their talents and strengths, are important parts of their leadership journey and personal brand.

In this chapter, you will:

- Learn about unique strengths
- Learn about the CliftonStrengths assessment and consider why it might be right for you
- Discover how your strengths can help you fulfill your purpose
- Explore how knowing your strengths can strengthen your brand
- Learn how strengths play a role in leadership

## What are Unique Strengths?

You were born with innate talents. When you become aware of those talents and work to develop them, they become your unique strengths. Unfortunately, some people go most of their lives unaware of what these innate talents are. I know many people who've made career decisions based solely on academics, sports scholarships, or the advice of well-meaning family members. They didn't think about or invest in their unique strengths. And they didn't consider what they wanted to contribute to the world. They didn't think about what really mattered to them.

I was one of those people. When I was a senior in high school, I wasn't sure what I wanted to study in college. My math, science, and english scores were very good, but I loved art classes. My guidance counselor and my parents believed that I was best suited to a career in engineering, based on academics alone. Art was perceived as something I could do in my spare time. These conversations about my future were meant to be supportive, but in hindsight, none of us really had all the tools necessary to make an informed decision.

I followed the advice and decided on civil engineering. During the winter of my second year, on a blustery February morning in Upstate New York, I stood freezing outside during my surveying class wondering why I'd chosen this. Was this really what I wanted to do? The answer was no. I spent the remainder of the year in a downward spiral, racking up debt and working toward a degree I knew I'd never use.

I began to explore other options and decided to take some graphic design classes to see if they were a better fit for me. They were! Having a love for both the art and the science of design, I decided to shift my focus to marketing. When I started my job at Dick's Sporting Goods, I was able to apply my talents to advertising and marketing, build an in-house department, and grow as a leader in the organization. I didn't know it then, but my innate talents paved the way for me. I was able to develop them into my unique strengths, which I carried forward into my marketing career.

## Focus on Improving Strengths

Some of my clients find themselves at a crossroads. They're in jobs they dislike or fields in which they don't feel they belong. Some want to reset their lives to focus on what they're meant to do. Like me, they made decisions early in their lives based on limited information.

Together, we go through the exercises in this book, and they also take the Gallup CliftonStrengths assessment. They become clear about what matters to them and discover their innate talents.

I've taken many assessments throughout my career. All can be valuable in some way if the person chooses to productively understand what the assessment is saying and grow from it. Fundamentally, though, I agree with strengths psychology and its focus on individual strengths. Focusing on strengths has proved to be meaningful and powerful in my personal and professional development, and I see the positive impact it has on my clients. When people understand their unique strengths, their world becomes clearer. The moment of understanding is priceless—a certain look comes across my clients' faces. They exhibit a childlike openness when they feel validated for who they are and the unique, innate talents they possess. It feels like a precious gift each time I get to experience that moment.

One time when I was at a networking event, I had an interesting conversation about strengths with an executive who was in her forties. We got chatting and she asked what I did for a living. I briefly described my journey from marketing executive to leadership coach (using my updated introduction!). I explained that I use the Gallup CliftonStrengths assessment as part of my coaching process. She told me she'd recently taken another assessment and was curious about CliftonStrengths. After I explained strengths psychology and the assessment to her, she said, "That's so refreshing! I have a list of five weaknesses I need to improve this year on the wall in my office. I walk in every morning, look at it, and feel angry. I would feel completely different if it were a list of my strengths!"

If you want to continue your journey of self-awareness, I encourage you find out exactly what your unique strengths are by taking the Gallup CliftonStrengths assessment and then working with a Gallup-certified coach to maximize your potential and turn your innate talents into powerful strengths.

## My Strengths

There is power in understanding strengths. When I learned my top five strengths, many things became clear. My successes, failures, deepest passions, and greatest frustrations were suddenly tied directly to my strengths in a way I never would have imagined. I realized that my strengths showed up throughout my life in different ways. And I found myself wishing I'd known about them earlier.

The CliftonStrengths assessment results are unique to each individual. The personalized strengths insights are based on the unique combination of your top five talent themes. Even though others might have some of the same talents as you, their description will differ from yours.

Here are my top five talent themes (referencing Gallup's general descriptions of each[2]) followed by my thoughts:

1. Individualization: I recognize the individual qualities in others and I find great joy in determining the best ways for people to work together. I value the differences and what makes each person unique.

This resonates with me. It clearly articulates what has mattered most to me throughout my career. Marketing is about understanding and reaching the target audience. Leadership is about identifying others' gifts and talents and helping others accomplish all they can. People, people, people.

2. Futuristic: I am inspired when I think about the future. I can create a vision and convey it to others to get them energized and excited about what could be.

I love thinking about what's possible. There have been times in my life I worried I might be restless. But learning I'm inspired when thinking about the future helped me understand my restlessness was about my desire to build toward a vision of the future. I can see it and work to bring others along. My husband cringes every time I say, "I have an idea I want to run past you." Buckle up!

3. Responsibility: I own what I do and what I commit to doing. I value honesty and loyalty in all my relationships.

When I think about how this strength has shown up in my life, I'm taken back to my work experiences, starting at McDonald's. I've always been committed to my responsibilities, and I expected to be held accountable for my actions as an employee. I'm also committed to doing my best for my family. I hate to let people down, even if it's unintentional. And I hate being let down or lied to.

4. ACHIEVER: When I take something on, I go all in. I take great satisfaction from working hard and I can't rest until everything is done correctly.

I easily lose track of time when I'm focused on something I really care about. I love change and I seek challenges. When someone tells me I can't do something, it's like fuel to me. I will find a way. If someone tells a person on my team that they can't do something, stand back—I'll do everything in my power to help that person achieve more than they thought was possible.

5. STRATEGIC: I can create various paths to move forward. I consider relevant data and anticipate potential roadblocks as I'm mapping out plans. When something does not go as planned, I analyze it, adapt, and then forge ahead.

Throughout my career, I've enjoyed solving problems. I love to build teams, processes, and procedures that help people. I love to find a way when others think there is no way. There is always a way.

## Linking Strengths and Purpose

One of my clients was feeling stalled in his career. He felt he'd followed all the rules, and he'd moved up the corporate ladder to a leadership position in a manufacturing company. He was passionate about the product but felt as if something was missing from his work and life. He wanted to propose a radical change in the product to better serve customers, or possibly create a spin-off business that would put him in direct contact with customers. His knowledge of the industry and the product was second to none. He had a great deal to offer the industry—well beyond what his company was doing. When he completed the strengths assessment, he had the same kind of epiphany I had when I finished mine.

After he went through the exercises you've gone through in this book and completed the CliftonStrengths assessment, he had a clear picture of his brand. He knew what mattered to him and had defined his purpose. He quickly realized that he had the strengths necessary to take the bold step he desired. He'd previously focused on his weaknesses, and this created self-doubt. Through the self-discovery process, he recognized that he was limiting himself to the role in his company instead of opening himself up to the possibility of fulfilling a greater purpose. With clarity on his purpose and what mattered to him, and armed with his strengths, he forged ahead confidently and created a complementary business that served the needs of the industry. He's now writing blogs based on his expertise, training industry leaders, and codeveloping products to better serve customers.

Linking your strengths to your purpose is powerful. If you identified any barriers in Chapter 2 related to confidence or skills when asked, "What are your greatest barriers to success?" you might consider taking the assessment to learn how you can leverage your strengths to fulfill your purpose.

## Your Strengths and Your Brand

When you know your strengths, you can integrate them into your description of yourself. For instance, I often refer to my futuristic strength when talking with my business partners or clients. We work in the business of envisioning a powerful future, so I love to leverage that strength.

Sometimes talking about your strengths can help others understand you better. As you bravely forge ahead to lead with authenticity and purpose, it can be helpful to let those around you know that you're using all the power of your strengths to achieve your goals. Sharing your strengths with your team, and encouraging them to share and apply their own, builds camaraderie and acceptance of what makes each of us unique.

Knowing your strengths creates a deeper sense of self-awareness and adds another dimension to your brand.

## Your Unique Strengths and the Leadership Gap

Clients frequently ask me, "Is there a combination of strengths that makes for a great leader?" The answer is no. There isn't a magical formula of strengths that identifies who will be a great leader and who won't.

The CliftonStrengths assessment isn't meant to identify *if* you have leadership strengths—it's meant to help you understand what your strengths are so you can lead.

The authentic leaders I've had the opportunity to work with have a variety of strengths. Each one has achieved the respect of many, but their styles are completely different. Their brands are their own. Each one approaches their business and manages their teams in ways that leverage their unique strengths. If they tried to model the behaviors of others or follow a cookie-cutter leadership-strengths profile, I'm certain they wouldn't be as successful. Why? Because it would be difficult to maintain a leadership style in an attempt to mimic *other's* strengths. A leadership gap would eventually be exposed in the inauthentic leader. Remaining authentic and leveraging *their own* strengths gives leaders the best advantage.

## Your Unique Strengths: Summary

The Gallup CliftonStrengths assessment, built on positive psychology and decades of research, is something to consider taking if you elect to go further down the path of your self-awareness journey.

Identifying your strengths can help you gain the tools and confidence you need to fulfill your purpose, particularly if you've identified barriers through the exercises. Your innate talents turn into strengths when you choose to invest in them. This decision starts with an awareness of those talents.

Knowing your strengths can help you enhance the description of your brand. And sharing your strengths in a team environment fosters an appreciation for the unique contributions of others.

There isn't a specific combination of strengths that indicates leadership success. Rather, you leverage the power of your strengths to lead authentically.

*To learn more about the CliftonStrengths assessment and gain access to it, visit https://www.gallupstrengthscenter.com/.*

## Chapter 11

# Now What?

*You will either step forward into growth or you will step back into safety.*

Abraham Maslow

Much of this book has been spent looking in the rearview mirror. The discovery exercises in this book have provided you with a roadmap. This map can be revisited and modified as things change in your life.

Now it's time to look through the windshield. You know what matters. And you know how authentically you're leading and living your brand today—or if you're not. You now have what's required to take action.

You have the power and potential to lead. It is inside you. You can lead by taking control of your words and actions to ensure they are in alignment with what matters deeply to you and are a clear reflection of your personal brand. Living your brand and leading with authenticity and purpose is a lifelong project. It starts today. Living your authentic brand isn't about becoming a different person. It's about becoming more of who you really are.

Your nexus statement is a starting point. You have created a statement that summarizes who you are and embodies what matters to you (as identified in your Venn Diagram). You can start your authentic brand journey by sharing your nexus statement with others. Using one of the examples from Chapter 4, the nexus statement, "I'm a teacher and mentor—I empower others," tells people in your personal and professional life what matters to you and helps them see what you can do for the world. Your nexus statement can be shared in interviews to help prospective employers know more about you, in discussions with your leader about your work in your current role or when seeking a new role, and it can be discussed in any situation with family, friends or others with whom you wish to have a more meaningful relationship.

Some of my clients elect to share their full Venn Diagram of core principles with their families and/or teams. You may decide that it's important to share yours as well. It can be helpful to you and those who matter most to you to discuss your personal, professional, and aspirational core principles. In a healthy personal relationship, knowing what matters to someone and what they aspire to be creates a deeper connection and support system. In a professional setting, when employees know where a leader is headed, they're more inclined to want to jump on board and get on the bus, so to speak. They may be energized by the aspirations and want to align their efforts toward the same end. And if not, they should be true to what matters to themselves and get on another bus.

Next, share your promises with the people you identified that matter most to you in your personal and professional relationships. It's important that they know what they can expect from you. When appropriate, help them understand that you've realized some things through this process and are committed to delivering on your promises. Some of your personal conversations may be particularly meaningful if you're committing to something new or changing something you've identified is important. Take the time to explain why keeping these promises matters to you. In a professional setting, you can share your promises with others frequently when committing to deadlines, contributing to a project, or assisting someone in a meaningful way. It doesn't have to be a big revelation, unless you want it to be–it can simply be shared in day-to-day contact and through consistent actions.

Your purpose statement tells others what you intend to do for the world. It summarizes your gifts and what you desire to achieve—your reason for being. This can be used on a resume and in your profile description on social media platforms. I've even seen some people use it in their email signature or on a business card. One of my clients created a screensaver with their purpose statement. It served as a daily reminder, it energized him, and it was seen by others, which often prompted great conversations! Another client put it on her bathroom mirror, so she started each day with her purpose in mind.

As you begin to share more of your authentic self, be sure you're leveraging your social media platforms to share, like, and create content that embodies who you are and what matters to you. If the picture of you hasn't been clear up to this point, it will become clear as you show others what is important to you through your social media activity.

Take charge of your description if you are in a situation where someone doesn't get it quite right. It's another great opportunity to share your nexus statement, your purpose statement, or some element of what matters to you that fits the situation. For example, if you are introduced in a professional setting simply by your name and title, like the example from Chapter 5, "This is Beth. She's a web designer," take the opportunity to continue the conversation with the new person you've just met and share a bit more about yourself. If you were Beth, you might follow the introduction with something like, "It's really great to meet you. I'm very excited to collaborate with you on this project. I'm really passionate about ensuring our customers have the best possible experience on our website." This will open up a richer dialogue and allow you to share more about yourself in future conversations.

Seek every opportunity to step up and lead. As I've covered in this book, leadership can begin at any age and is not defined by title.

Through the exercises, you've identified the leaders who have impacted you in your life. Now, it's time to be clear about the obligation you have to lead–to be an impactful person for others. If your actions inspire someone to do more, become more, learn more, and achieve more, you're a leader. When you begin to lead, you'll get noticed. You will influence others. You will make a difference.

You'll find as you experience more throughout your lifetime that other things begin to matter and become part of you, and therefore part of your brand. What matters in your life will continue to expand and contract as you seek to fulfill your purpose, deliver on your promises, and behave in a manner that is consistent with your principles. Believe in your brand, leverage your strengths, take responsibility for your impact on those around you. And then, as you *just do you*, you'll fill the leadership gap.

# Key Takeaways, Part Four

## YOUR TIME TO LEAD

- Leadership isn't about title, position, or power. Anyone can step up and be a leader. The world needs authentic leaders, leaders who are true to themselves and purpose driven
- The real-life examples shared throughout this book illustrate the influence of authentic leaders and the positive ripple effects they create through their interactions with others. Conversely, the inauthentic leaders who do harm, intentionally or unintentionally, leave people floundering in their wake
- Throughout your leadership journey, be open to lifelong learning. In doing so, you'll face new experiences and meet new people who can teach you something unexpected. Embrace your failures along the way and choose to fail forward. When you do this, you'll see that failures are simply opportunities to learn. And as a leader, when you help others overcome failures, you'll help them fail forward as well
- When the time comes, be willing to be the outlier. Experiences and people will challenge your brand. You'll

need to decide when to step up and shine authentically in those situations. It will be difficult, but the reward will be great. Stay on course toward your True North. Stay true to you

- It's up to you to choose how to proceed from here. You may want to continue on your self-awareness journey and take an assessment, such as Gallup CliftonStrengths. Or you may have some specific challenges you need to address. Find the resources that resonate with you and that align with your brand. I recommend several in the next chapter. Some books and methodologies will feel right and others won't. Be discerning in your quest to build your skills

**Now is your time to become the leader you were meant to be—maybe the leader you wish you had.**

## If You Like What You've Read

Like every other author, reader reviews make my world go round. It helps other people decide whether a book is right for them. So, do it for them, if not for me. :-) Please consider leaving an honest review where you bought the book. My thanks in advance.

# Recommended Reading

> *Live as if you were to die tomorrow. Learn as if you were to live forever.*
>
> Mahatma Gandhi

An endless number of powerful and inspiring books and resources are available to you as you continue your leadership journey. Keep learning and keep challenging yourself. It's likely you'll find some material that resonates with you and some that doesn't. The most important thing is to stay true to your authentic self—to your personal brand—and leverage your learnings to hone your skills and knowledge.

Think about what you noted in terms of developmental needs when completing the brand assessment in Chapter 6. Then consider the following books or resources and take the next step on your learning journey.

These are a few of my personal favorites, not in any particular order. I've included brief descriptions of why they might be helpful to you.

### If you've uncovered something that you're committed to changing . . .

. . . consider *The Power of Habit: Why We Do What We Do in Life and Business* by Charles Duhigg. This book will give you a greater understanding of the human brain and why you've developed certain habits. It's one of my all-time favorites on the science of habits, and the stories that Duhigg shares are powerful examples of dynamic change that can occur in people and organizations—even when deep-rooted habits have been formed.

If you want to understand more about how good and bad leadership experiences impact your psyche and how to build skills for successful leadership . . .

. . . read *Leaders Eat Last: Why Some Teams Pull Together and Others Don't* by Simon Sinek. I'm a huge Simon Sinek fan. This was the first book I read after leaving an extremely challenging and toxic work environment, and it was exactly what the doctor ordered. It connects science and emotion in a way I hadn't previously understood. Rich stories from people in business and the military demonstrate how successful teams can be when there's a "Circle of Safety." It's a fantastic journey.

If you discovered that you're displaying behaviors that may be diminishing others' abilities, or if you work for a leader who does this . . .

. . . consider *Multipliers: How the Best Leaders Make Everyone Smarter* by Liz Wiseman. Wiseman's research reveals that leaders fall on a spectrum between two categories: multiplier and diminisher. Generally speaking, Multipliers amplify the intelligence of the people around them. Diminishers do the opposite. She provides specific tactics and exercises to overcome certain behaviors and become a leader who is capable of multiplying talent, cultivating new ideas, and having a positive impact on organizations.

If you are committed to becoming an outlier and daring leader in your organization . . .

. . . *Dare to Lead: Brave Work. Tough Conversations. Whole Hearts* by Brene Brown is a must read. Brown utilizes decades of research and experiences inside hundreds of organizations to create a roadmap to success as a daring leader. She outlines four skillsets that can be taught, observed, and measured: Rumbling with Vulnerability, Living Our

Values, Braving Trust, and Learning to Rise. Brown's stories, humor, empirical data, and practical wisdom create an amazing reader journey that will cause you to dig deep and teach you how to become a daring leader.

If you're seeking to improve your personal and professional relationships by building trust and delivering on promises . . .

. . . read *The Speed of Trust: The One Thing That Changes Everything* by Stephen M.R. Covey. We all value our most trusted relationships. Covey not only explains the economics of trust, but also shows how to cultivate trust in yourself, your relationships, and the stakeholders in your organization. His research and practical examples demonstrate how trust has the power to create unparalleled success.

If you're interested in learning about authentic, purpose-driven leaders who succeeded when others around them failed . . .

. . . you'll want to read *Great by Choice* by Jim Collins and Morten T. Hansen. Nine years of research and amazing case studies that vividly illustrate what makes the world's best leaders and companies thrive even in the most uncertain and chaotic times make this an invaluable book for leaders. Collins and Hansen compared companies that started from a position of vulnerability and rose to become great with companies that faced a similar set of extreme circumstances and failed. Using the results, they uncovered the factors that allowed the successful leaders and companies to thrive.

If your work conflicts with your purpose and principles and you're ready to listen to your inner voice . . .

. . . consider *When to Jump: If the Job You Have Isn't the Life You Want* by Mike Lewis. This is an inspirational book in which the author shares his personal journey from having a prestigious corporate job to becoming a professional squash player. It also includes more than forty other personal stories of people who decided to follow their inner voice and make the jump. Jumping isn't easy—it takes courage and perseverance. This is a must-read for anyone who's in a rut and desires to make their purpose a reality.

When you're serious about turning your purpose into a business . . .

. . . try *Business Model Generation: A Handbook for Visionaries, Game Changers, and Challengers* by Alexander Osterwalder and Yves Pigneur. This isn't your traditional management or business strategy book. Highly visual and engaging exercises walk you through the process of building a solid business model. The authors replace outdated models with innovative design thinking that seeks to create value for companies, customers, and communities. Their process is organized and presented in a step-by-step manner that aims to help individuals and teams understand the complex architecture of business.

If you recognized that your presence needs a boost . . .

. . . read *The Energy Bus: 10 Rules to Fuel Your Life, Work, and Team with Positive Energy* by Jon Gordon. Gordon takes the reader on a journey by using a fable to illustrate his ten rules. He has created characters who embody many of the emotions and challenges we all encounter at some point in our lives. The fable gives the reader actionable tools to create more positive energy in all aspects of their lives. Positive energy is infectious and produces powerful results. I recommend this for a light, easy read that will put a smile on your face, a spring in your step, and a renewed focus on showing up with positivity.

When you're ready to challenge the status quo in your organization and step up and lead, regardless of where you are now . . .

. . . consider *Linchpin: Are You Indispensable?* by Seth Godin. This book busts many myths regarding various business models. Godin presents the stark reality of the changing workforce and the new expectations that require people to look at their roles differently. He urges the reader to make a choice, to take the road less traveled and stand out, to become a linchpin. Godin believes there's genius in all of us and that the opportunity to stand out is available to anyone who decides to step up and change their life for the better. It's not the easy choice, or the safe choice, but it's the only way to become indispensable.

### If you want to build leadership skills for your multigenerational workplace . . .

. . . read *The Remix: How to Lead and Succeed in the Multigenerational Workplace*, by Lindsey Pollak. Pollak dives deep into each generation's unique attributes and workstyle preferences and the need for organizations to maintain and maximize their diverse workforce. She covers topics such as communication, training, mentoring, networking, and even workspace layout. Each example is supported with data and stories that help create a picture of what this evolved work environment could be like—if more companies embraced a remix.

### If you wish to learn more about leveraging your strengths to be a more effective leader . . .

. . . read *Strengths Based Leadership* by Tom Rath and Barry Conchie. Supported by decades of research, Gallup reveals that the three keys to being a more effective leader are knowing your own strengths, investing in the strengths of others, and getting the right people with complementary strengths on your team. The book also includes actionable ideas for leading others based on their unique strengths. To learn your own strengths, take the CliftonStrengths assessment, https://www.gallupstrengthscenter.com/.

### If you identified some people who need to be written in or out of your next chapter . . .

. . . read *The Power of the Other* by Dr. Henry Cloud. A psychologist and best selling author, Dr. Cloud combines stories and case studies to illustrate the power people have over others. He emphasizes that exceptional performance and satisfaction comes from the right kind of positive interpersonal relationships. Those relationships have the power to fuel personal growth or diminish us.

For more leadership and personal development books, videos, and articles, visit https://danelipartners.com/home/influences-resources/.

# Acknowledgements

If I were to truly acknowledge everyone who helped me fill the pages of this book, I would have to list all the people who matter most to me in my personal and professional life–many of whom are already mentioned in the stories and experiences I shared. I'm fortunate to have many influencers and leaders who believed in me and helped me throughout my lifetime.

First, I'd like to thank my business partner David Casullo for encouraging me to write a book by telling me repeatedly, "You have a book inside you!" He knows I can't resist a challenge. To my other business partner, Neil Rosenbaum, I owe you and your eternal optimism a great debt. You made me and David believe the three of us could take the leap and start a business together. I am grateful for every day we work toward our aligned purposes. It's a dream come true.

I want to thank all the survey respondents who so openly and honestly shared their stories and experiences. You are leaders and I know each one of you will accomplish all that you desire.

To my son Andrew and daughter Jessica, you are my heart and soul. You inspire me every day with your kindness, unique personalities, and passion for what you do. There is no greater joy in my life than to see you both become the amazing adults and leaders you are. I love you more than words can express.

Most importantly, thank you to Bill, my husband and soulmate, for your constant love and support. Regardless of what I take on, you are by my side cheering me on and encouraging me. You deliver the perfect balance of motivation and empathy—exactly what's needed in the moment. I could not have asked for a better partner to share this life with. I love you now and forever.

# About the Author

Photo Credit: Keegan Evans Photography

Lisa King was a senior marketing and branding leader, C-suite executive, and managing partner/consultant for global consumer products companies for nearly three decades prior to chasing her dream of launching a business. Lisa's true passion for developing brands, culture, teams, and leaders to drive business success is the reason she is the cofounder and president of Daneli Partners. She is also a Gallup certified strengths coach. Her knowledge of professional branding and strengths development empower leaders to clarify what matters and create a successful personal brand that drives professional success. Lisa lives in Skaneateles, New York with her husband, Bill.

Danelipartners.com

LinkedIn https://www.linkedin.com/in/lisa-king-99004223/

 instagram.com/lkrun4life

*If you enjoyed* ***Just Do You****, please consider leaving a brief review on the website or with the retailer where you bought the book.*

*Reviews are is very important to every author. Your feedback doesn't have to be long or detailed. Just a sentence saying what you enjoyed.*

*Please accept my thanks if this is something you'd like to do.*

# Notes

## Chapter 1: Authentic Leadership

1. Gallup, Inc., "*State of the American Workplace*", (2017) Executive Summary, page 8. (Gallup developed *State of the American Workplace* using data collected from more than 195,600 U.S. employees via the Gallup Panel and Gallup Daily tracking in 2015 and 2016, and more than 31 million respondents through Gallup's Q12 Client Database. First launched in 2010, this is the third iteration of the report.) Accessed November 2018, https://www.gallup.com/workplace/ 238085/state-american-workplace-report-2017.aspx.
   workplace-report-2017.aspx.
2. Gallup, Inc., *"How Millennials Want to Work and Live"*, (2016), Executive Summary, page 10. (The findings in this report are based on accumulated Gallup data derived from the Gallup Panel, Gallup Daily tracking, Gallup's employee engagement and customer engagement databases, and the Gallup-Healthways Well-Being Index.) https://www.gallup.com/workplace/238073/millennials-work-live.aspx
3. Gallup, Inc., *"Gallup's Approach to Culture; Building a Culture That Drives Performance"*, (2018), The Five Drivers of Culture, page 15. https://www.gallup.com/workplace/ 232682/culture-paper-2018.aspx

## Chapter 2: Determine What Matters

1. David Casullo, *Leading the High Energy Culture* (McGraw Hill, 2012)

## Chapter 3: Authentic Branding

1. Newman's Own Foundation, *About Us*, accessed November 2018, http:// newmansownfoundation.org/about-us/history/

## Chapter 4: Connect to Who You Are

1. Vozza, Stephanie. "Personal Mission Statements of 5 CEOs (and Why You Should Write One Too)" (Fast Company, February 25, 2014.) https://www.fastcompany.com/3026791/personal-mission-statements-of-5-famous-ceos-and-why-you-should-write-one-too, accessed July 31, 2019.
2. Vozza, "Personal Mission Statements of 5 Famous CEOs."
3. Vozza, "Personal Mission Statements of 5 Famous CEOs."

## Chapter 7: Identify Conflicts

1. Sarah Young, "Gut Feelings Really Do Stop You Making Mistakes, Study Finds," The Independent, March 23, 2018, https://www.independent.co.uk/life-style/gut-feelings-instinct-stop-mistakes-brain-signal-influence-emotions-study-findings-a8270611.html, accessed July 31, 2019.
2. CareerBuilder, "More Than Half of Employers Have Found Content on Social Media That Caused Them NOT to Hire a Candidate, According to Recent Career-Builder Survey," August 9, 2018, https://www.prnewswire.com/news-releases/more-than-half-of-employers-have-found-content-on-social-media-that-caused-them-not-to-hire-a-candidate-according-to-recent-careerbuilder-survey-300694437.html, accessed July 31, 2019.
3. Robert McGuire, "How Many Freelancers Are There," Nation1099, July 16, 2018, https://nation1099.com/gig-economy-data-freelancer-study/, accessed July 31, 2019.

## Chapter 10: Your Unique Strengths

1. Gallup, Inc., *Positive Psychology*, accessed November 2018, https://my.gallup.com/_Help/HelpCenter?appName=Portal&tile=HELP_TILE_HEADING_CLIFTONSTRENGTHS_CLIFTONSTRENGTH&topic=HELP_PERSONALITY_CS_Q&p=1833497077
2. Gallup, Inc., *The 34 Ways to Describe What You Naturally Do Best*, accessed November 2018, https://www.gallup.com/cliftonstrengths/en/253715/34-cliftonstrengths-themes.aspx

CPSIA information can be obtained
at www.ICGtesting.com
Printed in the USA
BVHW041017290722
643352BV00007B/58